Famous Biographies for Young People

FAMOUS

BASEBALL STARS

FAMOUS
BASEBALL STARS

by Bill Gutman

ILLUSTRATED WITH PHOTOGRAPHS

Dodd, Mead & Company · New York

ISBN: 0-396-06776-X
Library of Congress Catalog Card Number: 72-12542
Printed in the United States of America
by Vail-Ballou Press, Inc., Binghamton, N. Y.

FOR BETH

CONTENTS

Illustrations follow page 84

CONTENTS

FAMOUS

BASEBALL STARS

JOHN PETER (HONUS) WAGNER

The Dutchman

[1874–1955]

THE WHITE-HAIRED man paused for a moment, chewing thoughtfully on a big wad of tobacco. He spat. Then he looked at his three youthful admirers, all wearing the uniform of the Pittsburgh Pirates, as did he.

"Did I tell you about the time I was playing shortstop and this dog runs out onto the field?" he said in an old, cracking voice.

All three players exchanged glances. What was the old man going to come up with now?

"Well, just as this mutt comes out, the ball is hit toward me and the runner on second breaks for third. Wouldn't you know it, Fido scoops up the ball. Now this is a situation they don't teach you about in baseball school. I said to myself, 'Honus, you ain't gonna let a little dog stop you from making this play.' So I picked up the dog, ball and all, and threw them both over to third. The third baseman tagged the runner and the dog held the ball. But we got our man . . . and I guess that little dog got an assist, too."

The three young baseball players broke out in a laugh.

"No kidding, Honus," one said.

"Honest, coach," exclaimed another.

"I wouldn't kid you fellows. A lot of funny things happened back then."

The old man waddled off, in the direction of another group of players, presumably to tell another tale. Though he had bowed legs and looked a little weary and unsteady, he nevertheless held himself erect, his ruddy features, prominent jaw, and hooked nose recognizable to all those around the Pittsburgh area. Only a few old-timers remembered seeing him play. But those who were lucky enough to have seen Honus Wagner play baseball knew they'd seen the greatest shortstop of all time, and one of the greatest ever to play the game.

As for the youngsters, they just enjoyed having Honus around. He had come back to the Pirates as a coach in 1933. At that time he was getting ready to celebrate his sixtieth birthday, so the Dutchman, as he was called, goes back a long way.

Honus remained active as a Pirate coach until 1951. By then, he was nearing eighty, still as lively as they come, always ready with a quip or story, or a tale from the past. You couldn't always be sure when Honus Wagner was telling the truth or stretching it a bit, but you knew that the old man had seen a lot of baseball in his lifetime.

That lifetime began for John Peter Wagner on February 24, 1874, in Carnegie, Pennsylvania. The town was called Mansfield back then, and was right in the middle of the state's coal mining belt, an area of the country that continues to produce top-flight athletes. Football's Joe Namath is from Beaver Falls, and basketball's Pistol Pete Maravich was born in Aliquippa, just to name two of the more famous Pennsylvania stars of today.

In Honus' time, as today, the principal occupation in the region was mining. And the Wagners were a mining family, Bavarian immigrants who worked from dawn to dusk in the hot, dangerous mines, trying to scratch out a meager living for their families.

There were nine children in the Wagner family, plenty of mouths to feed. Everyone had to chip in and do his share.

That's why young Honus started going down into the mines when he was twelve. There he loaded coal at the rate of seventy cents a ton. Since he could only load one ton per day, that meant just $3.50 a week. But every little bit helped. There were many days when he didn't really feel like going down to the mines, especially when some of his friends would approach him with bats and gloves.

"How about playing some baseball with us today, Hans?"

"Sorry, fellows," was the sad answer, "but I've got to work today."

The one thing that the hard work did was develop Honus' arms and shoulders. When he did find time to play ball with his friends, he hit the ball farther than anyone. And his big, strong hands gobbled up everything in sight, no matter where he played. When the boys in the neighborhood arranged a game with some other boys, the word was this: "We can win if we have Honus."

It was always a battle to get young Wagner out of the mines and onto the diamond. But they got him out more and more as time went on. The reason was that Honus was slowly falling in love with the game.

"It's a funny thing," he said in later years. "At first the money was more important to me. I didn't want to lose that payday. But slowly things changed. Before long, it was base-ball that was more important. The money didn't matter any more."

Still, the idea of playing professional baseball in those days wasn't very appealing, and for awhile Honus thought about following in the footsteps of one of his brothers and becom-ing a barber. But there was no way it could happen. The bar-bering idea ended in 1895 when the Steubenville team of the International League offered Honus a chance to play profes-sionally at the salary of $35.00 a week.

"The first week's pay didn't last long," Honus said with a smile. "After all, I was just a poor boy from Pennsylvania. I had to buy a glove, some baseball shoes, and my own uni-form. That left me three bucks spending money."

But again, money didn't matter. Honus was doing what he liked, and before long the Dutchman began to make his pres-ence felt. The records from those early years are difficult to find, but in forty-four games for Steubenville, Honus batted a cool .402. He quickly showed he wasn't fooling around. He was for real.

The Dutchman was a shortstop that first year, the position he'd later play in the majors. But he was a versatile performer who could play anywhere. He once advised youngsters not to settle on a position until they reached the age of eighteen. That way, they could develop all around skills. And Wagner certainly had all the skills.

He was a brawny 5′ 11″, weighing two hundred pounds, with much of his strength concentrated in the chest and shoulders. He had bow legs, but they didn't hamper his movement. He had grace and style for a big man, and his hands were like glue, his arms very strong.

At the plate, he stood deep in the batter's box on the right side. He held the bat down at the end and crouched low, like a cat ready to pounce. The pounce in his case was a short, compact swing, that sometimes looked like a lunge but which was deadly accurate. The batting style wasn't classic, but the results were.

Honus was a vagabond in 1895. After tearing up the league with Steubenville, he played with Mansfield in the Ohio State League, with Adrian in the Michigan State League, and finally with Warren in the Iron-Oil League. Baseball was surely different then! The next year he batted .349 with Paterson, New Jersey, of the Atlantic League, and midway through the 1897 season he moved up to the Louisville team of the National League. Honus Wagner was in the majors.

Early in his rookie season, Honus belted a long hit against the tough Baltimore Orioles. It looked like a triple. But Jack Doyle, the Oriole first baseman, gave the rookie a shot with his hip, shortstop Hughie Jennings made him run a mile wide at second, and John McGraw blocked the bag at third, then knocked the wind out of the youngster when he tagged him in the stomach.

"What's the matter with you, Hans?" roared Louisville manager Fred Clarke. "If you let those guys get away with that stuff, they'll run you right out of the league!"

Legend has it that Honus belted another long drive in that same game. This time he charged around the bases like a Brahma bull. He knocked Doyle on his seat at first, shoved Jennings out of the way at second, and barreled into McGraw at third, spikes first. It makes a great baseball story, and there must be some truth in it, because few people ever got in the Dutchman's way again.

Honus played a lot of first base and outfield in those first few seasons. He hit .359 for Louisville in 1899, and then, in

1900, the franchise was shifted to Pittsburgh. Honus Wagner was delighted. He was coming home.

But he was by no means a stranger to baseball fans. By 1897, there was a Honus Wagner perfecto, put out by a cigar manufacturer, as well as a beer named after him. That happened while he was still at Paterson.

Once in Pittsburgh, Honus was happy. The fans knew he was from the area and came out in droves to watch him play. *Come on, Honus. Belt one outta here for the boys back home!*

Hey, Hans, do it like you used to in Mansfield!

Those cries weren't uncommon in Pittsburgh, and the Dutchman responded. Playing mostly in the outfield, he rapped out 201 hits in 141 games, and finished by leading the league in hitting with a .381 average, the highest of his career, making him the first batting champion of the twentieth century. It was also the first of eight National League batting crowns the Dutchman would win, a record that still stands.

Honus played shortstop for the first time in 1903, and won another batting title with a .355 average. It was also the first year that the Pirates won the pennant, making Honus a part of baseball history. He participated in the very first World Series.

In 1900, a man named Ban Johnson had become tired of the National League monopoly. He thought there was room for another league, so he started one, called it the American League, and promptly raided the older loop for talent. It was the first of many sports-talent wars which still rage today in basketball and hockey.

Salaries weren't high in those days, and many of the top players were easily induced to jump leagues, giving the American League an equal footing within two or three years, and setting up the championship playoff called the World Series. If Hans Wagner had been a different kind of man, he might not have been playing for Pittsburgh in that first interleague clash.

The Dutchman was one of the players approached by the American League in 1903. The National had a salary limit of $2,400 then, and many players with lesser abilities than the Dutchman were getting more money for switching leagues. Wagner was approached by Clark Griffith, manager of the New York Highlanders, forerunner of the Yankees.

"I'd like you to play for the Highlanders next year," Griffith said flatly.

Honus stuck out his prominent jaw.

"Not interested," he said.

With that, Griffith took out a briefcase, and slowly began counting. When he was finished, there were twenty $1,000 bills sitting on the table, crisp and green and new. Honus had never seen that much money in his life. He swallowed hard.

"Like I said, Mr. Griffith, I'm not interested."

It was a combination of loyalty and a desire to continue playing near his home town that made Honus refuse. Plus the fact that he never had a burning love of money. When he became one of the great stars of the game, he achieved a yearly salary of $10,000. That was in 1909. Every year after that, a recurring scene was repeated in the office of Pirate owner Barney Dreyfuss.

"What do you think you'll want this year?" Dreyfuss would ask.

"Same as last year," the Dutchman would reply without hesitation.

Dreyfuss would then give Honus a blank contract, which he quickly signed. Then the Pirate owner would fill in the rest, with the salary the same as the previous year. He didn't reward Honus when he refused to jump leagues, and he didn't reward him for his play or drawing power in those later years. Many people told Honus to press for more money, but the Dutchman was satisfied. No one in his family ever dreamed of earning as much as $10,000. It was enough.

There were other instances of Honus' declining to opt for the almighty dollar. One year Ty Cobb, the American League's equivalent of Wagner, asked the Dutchman if he wanted to barnstorm the vaudeville circuit for $1,000 per week.

"I ain't no actor, Ty," Honus answered. "Thanks, anyway."

The first World Series was a dismal failure as far as the Pirates were concerned. With the reputation of the older league at stake, Pittsburgh was out to bury the Red Sox. They ended up losing, five games to three. Honus didn't have a good Series. He got just six hits in twenty-seven at-bats for a .222 average. It was one of the few disappointments of his career.

But the Series didn't affect the Dutchman's performance during the next few years. He had batting averages of .349, .363, .339, .350, .354, and .339. In fact, he was to compile a better than .300 mark for seventeen consecutive seasons, a National League record that still stands. He also ran up a league mark of 720 stolen bases. The Dutchman could run, too.

He didn't hit too many homers, but he set a league record for triples with 252. Playing in the era of the dead ball, it wasn't easy to clout one over the wall. He sometimes said later that he often wished he had played with the lively ball; then he could have belted a few. With his strength, there's no doubt that he could have, too.

Whenever the Dutchman was challenged, he responded, especially when going up against the best. One example is his lifetime mark against the best pitcher in the National League, Christy Mathewson. Honus faced Big Six for more than fifteen years, and when it was over, he had compiled a .324 average against Matty, just five points below his lifetime mark of .329.

Then there was the 1909 World Series. In this one, the Pirates were going up against the Detroit Tigers, and their young star, Ty Cobb. Honus was thirty-five years old then, Cobb just twenty-three, but the comparisons were already being made. Ty was dynamite, a dedicated, fiery performer. Like Wagner, he hit to all fields, and like Wagner, he stole a lot of bases. Many thought he did it all just a little better than the Dutchman.

Early in the Series, Ty singled. When he got to first he looked down to second and hollered in the direction of Wagner, "Hey, Krauthead, I'm coming down on the first pitch." It was Ty's way of inciting the opposition into errors.

Honus flashed a faint smile.

"I'll be waiting," he said.

On the next pitch, Ty went. He came in to second, spikes flying. But Honus was there with the ball. He planted his feet, then planted the tag, ball first, square in Ty's mouth. Cobb was out, and left the field with a cut lip. He didn't razz the Dutchman for the rest of the Series.

When it was over, the Pirates had won, four games to three. Honus had eight hits in twenty-four at-bats for a .333 average, while Ty managed only .231. In addition, the 35-year-old Dutchman swiped six bases, a record which stood until 1967. Cobb, by contrast, had just two thefts. The old pro could still show a young upstart a thing or two.

But the 1909 season wasn't all glory for Honus. In fact, for the first time he thought about quitting. His legs began bothering him, a touch of arthritis that was to plague him the rest of his life. Some said he had picked it up as a boy in the dampness of the mines. At any rate, it started to slow him down a bit.

But there was still life in the Dutchman. Two years later, in 1911, he won his eighth and last batting crown with a .334 mark. He also drove home 108 runs that season in just 130 games. Not bad for a thirty-seven year old with bad legs. Two more .300 seasons followed, then the Dutchman slipped to .252 in 1914.

It wasn't fair to complain. Honus was now forty. But the Dutchman had always been a .300 hitter and the sudden decline came as a shock. He bounced back to .274 and .287 the next two seasons, but he'd never come all the way back again. The end was near.

In 1917, at the age of forty-three, Honus Wagner appeared in just seventy-four games for the Pirates. He made just sixty-one hits, giving him a total of 3,430 for his career, and he batted a mediocre .265—mediocre by his standards. It was time to hang up the spikes. The Dutchman didn't want to carry on any longer.

It wasn't until he was ready to retire that Honus married. His wife was a Pittsburgh girl named Bessie Smith, and the couple had two daughters, but no sons.

Always in good condition, Honus continued to play basketball and baseball for awhile, making tours with barnstorming teams. He also coached the two sports at Carnegie Tech for a short period of time. He owned a sporting goods store with another Pirate star, Pie Traynor.

But it was the inactivity that got to him. That's why he consented to climb back into uniform in 1933 as a Pirate coach. Once a shy and withdrawn young man, the older Wagner was talkative and outgoing. Besides telling a gamut of stories to his young admirers, he became a favorite speaker at banquets and dinners in the Pittsburgh area.

Honus Wagner enjoyed his life in baseball. He excelled at the game, but accepted the end of his playing days as inevitable. He then settled down to watch others play and help whenever he could.

Just how good was the Dutchman? Many think he was the best, others vote for Cobb, others for Babe Ruth. Ed Barrow, a man very close to all three, once said that Ruth was the best hitter, Cobb the greatest driving force, but Honus was the best all around. He could play anywhere.

When the old man died at age eighty-one in 1955, people who never saw him play, never even knew him, mourned his passing. That's how it is with legends. It's almost as if he's still in Pittsburgh today, wandering back and forth among the clusters of young players, spinning his baseball yarns by the dozen.

"The first time my old manager, Fred Clarke, told me to lay one down (bunt), I got a fat pitch and swatted a home run. Well, when I got back to the dugout, I thought Clarke was gonna kill me. So I said to him that I thought 'lay one down' meant 'lay on it.' He just nodded.

"Next time I came up, Clarke says to me, 'Lay one down, Dutch, okay?' Then he winked, 'Just like the last time.'"

No one stayed angry at Honus Wagner for long. He was just too good.

CHRISTOPHER MATHEWSON
Big Six

[1880–1925]

No ONE EVER had to teach Christy Mathewson how to throw a baseball. That came naturally. When Matty was just a youngster in the small town of Factoryville, Pennsylvania, he was already throwing his fastball past older, bigger boys, and even grown men.

They called him "Husk" then, a tribute to his size and maturity. One day in the summer of 1893, when he was thirteen, some men from the local semipro team asked Christy to pitch a game against their archrivals. The men had to swallow their pride to do it, but the regular pitcher had a sore arm and the only other hurler anyone could think of was "Husk" Mathewson. They all knew he could throw.

Young Matty did the job, all right. He had a blazing fastball, and had already developed a fine curve. After he won that first game, Matty was approached by the captain of the Factoryville team.

"That was some game you pitched today, Husk," the older man said. "Are you tired?"

Christy looked up modestly. He had just beaten a team of grown men, but he showed no outward excitement.

"Not a bit tired. I could pitch another game right now."

"Well, I didn't have a game in mind now. But I'd like you to pitch regularly for our team. How about it?"

"I'd be happy to pitch for you fellows," said Christy.

They paid Matty a dollar for that first game, making him a pro at thirteen. He'd be a pro for a long time. When the career of Christy Mathewson finally came to an end, he had won more games than any pitcher in National League history, setting records along the way that may never be broken. So great were his pitching skills that he was one of five players elected charter members of baseball's Hall of Fame when it opened in 1936.

Christy Mathewson was born in Factoryville on August 12, 1880. His father was a prosperous farmer and his mother had come from a well-to-do family, so life was good to the Mathewsons and their five children. They lived comfortably and never went without the necessities.

Matty was the oldest, but he did not feel he was someone special. From the outset, he was modest, courteous, and soft-spoken. There was never any arrogance or conceit in the youngster. He was always, in the truest sense, a gentleman.

His parents stressed education. They were aware of the changing times in America and knew that their children would have to be well educated to make their way in the world. Christy, as did all the Mathewson children, attended Keystone Academy, a private school that had been founded by his own grandmother.

Christy stayed at Keystone Academy right through high school. He studied and had fun, playing ball often and associating with other happy, trouble-free boys his age. He experienced none of the hardships and turmoil that characterized the early lives of so many of the ballplayers during that time.

Baseball for him wasn't a way out . . . it was just a way.

In fact, when he was only eight years old, he announced to his parents:

"I'm going to be a baseball player when I grow up. I'm going to play in the big leagues. You'll see, I'll be a pitcher, and a good one."

His parents didn't take him seriously. After all, in the 1880's and 90's, professional baseball was in its infancy, and the men who played it were usually hard-boiled ruffians, who enjoyed a good brawl as well as a good game.

But young Matty was serious, and when his talents developed at such an early age, his parents wondered if his earlier prediction might not come true. They began to hear stories about their son, such as the one when he was sixteen.

Christy was sitting in the grandstand at Scranton, Pennsylvania, watching two area teams play. One of the players recognized the boy and asked him to pitch. Matty put his bag of peanuts aside, climbed into a borrowed uniform, warmed up, and proceeded to win the game and strike out fifteen men!

Matty's reputation was growing. Fans began looking for the handsome youngster in the local semipro games. He was already full grown when he entered Bucknell University in 1898, a striking 6′ 2″, and 195 pounds. He had wispy blond hair which he was always pushing back off his forehead.

Bucknell was also in Pennsylvania, so Christy continued to pitch whenever he had the chance. In the summers, he earned up to two hundred dollars a month, his strong right arm dispatching rival batters with relative ease.

If his parents thought college life would end his dreams of being a ballplayer, they were wrong. He played both football and baseball at Bucknell, but in his mind, his singular ambition remained the same. There was one thing, however, that happened to Matty at Bucknell that he'd never be sorry for.

Her name was Jane Stoughton and she was a pretty, southern girl, with all the charm of the young ladies of that region. She was one of the most popular girls on the campus, but once she met Christy, she knew she'd found her man. When Jane asked Matty if he was going to be a ballplayer, he hedged.

"I don't know," he told her. "I like baseball, all right. But you can't play forever. I think I'd like to make forestry my life's work."

Whether he meant it or not is uncertain. It wasn't long after that he asked Jane to marry him. She said yes. She loved him very much, but she also said that she didn't want poverty to come between them. They'd marry as soon as Christy had some money to make them comfortable. After all, they were just students.

That did it. His love for Jane made the decision even easier. Now he knew what he'd do.

"We'll wait, Jane," he said. "But it won't be long. There's nothing wrong with making a living playing baseball. And I know I'll be successful. You wait and see."

In the summer of 1899, Christy signed to play for the Taunton club in the New England League.

It wasn't easy at Taunton. The team was terrible. They couldn't hit or field, and Christy lost game after game by scores of 2–1, 3–0, 3–2. When it all ended, he had won just two and lost twelve. But like most of Matty's experiences, he gained from it.

Taunton had a pitcher by the name of Williams. He wasn't really in Matty's class as a hurler, but he had a strange pitch that interested the young righthander. Williams threw it something like a curve, but the ball always took an odd and unpredictable route to the plate. He couldn't control it.

Christy watched Williams pitch. Instead of rotating his wrist upward to the sky, as most pitchers did on a regular curve, he rotated it downward. Christy tried it. The pitch moved. If he could only learn to control it, he'd have a pitch that would curve in to a right-handed batter and away from a lefty. The famous "fadeaway" pitch was about to be born.

Matty worked and worked on the new pitch. It began to come. Pretty soon he'd be able to throw it with accuracy. And pretty soon he'd be making his mark in the major leagues.

The next year, Christy started off with the Norfolk club of the Virginia League. He was throwing the fadeaway now, and with the rest of his arsenal, he mowed down Virginia League hitters at a fast clip. By mid-July, his manager, Phenom Smith, approached Christy with a big smile on his face.

"Guess what, Matty," he said.

Christy looked puzzled.

"You're going to be leaving us," the manager continued. "And you've got your pick. Philadelphia or New York."

Christy still said nothing. Finally, Smith began to explain. Both the Philadelphia Athletics and New York Giants were bidding for Matty's services. Matty balked. He knew Norfolk had a chance at the pennant. He had already won twenty games and lost just two, and he didn't want to walk out on all his teammates now.

"Listen, Matty," Smith said. "This is the chance of a lifetime. You go and you go now. They don't knock at the door forever. Make your pick and get going."

Christy thought it out very carefully. He knew about the

Philadelphia team. They were building a powerful ball club in the new American League. Connie Mack, the manager and owner, had bought some great players, including Napoleon Lajoie and Eddie Plank. The team would probably win a lot of games the next few years.

As for the Giants, in 1900, they were a rag-tag collection of nobodys. The team was owned by a politician named Andrew Freedman, and had had a succession of inept managers who couldn't put together a winning combination. Anyone with a choice would be out of his mind to pick the Giants. Christy thought it all over and told Phenom Smith of his decision.

"I want to get right in there and pitch. I figure I'll have a better chance of doing that with the Giants."

Even though Connie Mack had already sent money to bind the deal, Christy stuck to his decision. It would be the Giants, and he reported on July 17, 1900, to begin his big league career.

The first year was a terrible disappointment. The Giant manager, George Davis, didn't pitch Matty except for a few games in relief. The young righthander wondered if he'd made a mistake. He finished the year with an 0–3 record while appearing in just six games.

Matty returned to Bucknell after the season to resume his studies. He played football again and became the team's place-kicker. In fact, he was so good that Walter Camp named him to the All-America team, the first time a kicking specialist was so honored. But that was to be Matty's final year on the gridiron, and at Bucknell.

It was a strange twist when Matty didn't report to the Giants that spring. He was bought by the Cincinnati team. But the Redlegs wanted a pitcher named Amos Rusie, who was with the Giants. So before the season started, Matty was traded back to New York.

This time he was determined to make good. His future marriage to Jane depended on it. So did a lot of other things. He started his first game against the powerful Brooklyn Dodgers and emerged a 5–3 winner. It was his first major league victory and established him as one of the Giants' regular starting pitchers.

When the season ended, Matty was a twenty-game winner, finishing with a record of 20–17. Many of the losses were the fault of his teammates. They didn't get him any runs and made errors behind him in the field. But Matty never complained. He knew he could pitch and win now. Nothing else really mattered.

That included the 1902 season. It was a real disaster. Christy was a losing pitcher at 14–17. But his earned-run average was less than two runs per game. Plus the Giants had a new manager who promised to change everything.

His name was John J. McGraw, and he was a fighting, fiery leader who wanted a winning team. He told owner Freedman that he was the boss, no matter what, and Freedman agreed. McGraw started to build. First he went to Matty.

"Don't be discouraged, boy. You're my top pitcher and before long you're gonna be winning a whole lot of ball games."

McGraw was right. Matty reported to spring training in 1903 with his new bride, the former Jane Stoughton. Then he went to work. Before the season ended, he had won thirty ball games, losing just thirteen. Iron Man Joe McGinnity, another Giant hurler, won thirty-one that year, but the team didn't win the pennant.

The next year they did. Matty pitched in forty-eight games, won thirty-three of them, and dropped just twelve. With McGinnity winning thirty-five, there was no stopping McGraw and his New Yorkers. The only thing that tarnished the season was that John Tomlinson Brush, the new owner of the Giants, wouldn't let the club compete in the World Series. It was still a matter of choice in those days, and Brush didn't want anything to do with the American League. That would have to wait till next year.

In the meantime, Christy Mathewson was becoming one of the most beloved figures in the game. Many of the ballplayers in those days had little refinement or grace. Christy was one of the few college men in the sport. He took quite a ribbing from his teammates, and some fans and opponents, who would often shout:

"Come on, college boy, what's wrong?"

"Figure that one out, brains."

"You ain't so smart. How'd you get into college, anyway?"

But it didn't last long. People soon realized that this uncomplaining, quiet competitor was as much a fighter in his own way as anyone else.

Legend has it that a young ballplayer, seeing Matty pitch for the first time, looked out at the mound in awe.

"There's a big six," he said, referring to Christy's 6' 2" height.

"He's about the biggest six I ever saw," said another player.

Thus was born the name "Big Six," the handle newsmen and fans used in describing their hero. And Matty was worthy of the tag.

On the mound he was the boss. He had impeccable control, walking only about one batter a game. The rest he kept off balance with his fastball, curve, and mystifying fadeaway pitch. His handsome countenance and unassuming manner made him even more popular. And after the 1905 season, everyone in America knew who Big Six was.

That year, the Giants breezed to another pennant, Matty contributing thirty-one wins while losing just nine. This time the Giants played in the World Series, facing the powerful Philadelphia Athletics of Connie Mack, the team Mathewson might have been playing for had he chosen differently.

The Series opened in Philadelphia with the 25-year-old Matty facing the A's ace, Eddie Plank. When Matty retired the A's on just four pitches in the first, it looked like it was going to be a good day. The Giants got a pair of runs in the fifth and one more in the ninth. They led, 3–0.

Philadelphia could do nothing with Matty. He continued his mastery until the final out and finished with a four-hit shutout to give the Giants the series lead. After Chief Bender shut out the Giants for the A's in game two, Matty returned to the mound in the third game.

This time it was even easier. The Giants scored early, and continued scoring, finishing with nine runs, while the Athletics got absolutely nothing. The amazing Mathewson shut them out again on four hits. He fanned nine and walked one, his first base on balls in eighteen innings. The score of the third game was 9–0.

MATTY DOES IT AGAIN read one headline.

BIG SIX MAKES SERIES HISTORY said another.

But what they didn't know was that Matty wasn't through yet. Iron Man McGinnity followed Christy's lead and shut out the A's in game four. Now the Giants had a 3–1 lead and had to win just once more. No one figured McGraw would pitch Matty after just one day of rest.

"How do you feel?" the tough little manager asked his ace.

"Fine," answered Matty. He was ready to go again.

"I want you to pitch today and wrap this thing up," McGraw said. "Can you do it?"

"I'll sure try."

The old Polo Grounds was bursting at the seams that day as some 27,000 fans squeezed in to see Matty pitch. He was their hero, all right, and they hoped he'd win it. But after two shutouts, they wondered how he could possibly do it again. With Chief Bender his opponent, it wouldn't be easy.

In the opening innings, it looked as if the A's were going to get him. They put men on base in each of the first three innings, but the big righthander went to work and pitched out of trouble.

Then in the fifth, the Giants got a run to break the ice. In the eighth they got another, Matty scoring it himself after walking. The rest was up to him. In the final three innings, a tired Christy Mathewson faced just nine men. Only one could get the ball out of the infield. That's how good Matty was.

When the game ended, the Polo Grounds fans went wild. They gathered outside the Giants' clubhouse and screamed for their heroes, so the dramatic McGraw produced them one by one. Matty got the loudest cheer of all, one that could probably be heard all the way back to Philadelphia.

And he deserved it. Matty had pitched three full games, twenty-seven innings, and hadn't given up a single run. He allowed only fourteen hits in three games, struck out eighteen, and walked just one man. It was the most amazing performance by a pitcher in World Series history. No one before or since ever duplicated his feat.

Big Six was the toast of the baseball world. He was just twenty-five years old. It didn't seem that there were too many more worlds to conquer. But even at his moment of jubilation, Matty paused to give credit to others.

"A pitcher doesn't win unless he has a good team behind him," he told the press. "And I was lucky enough to have a great team behind me in the Series."

The next year, good luck seemed to abandon the Giant star. He contracted diptheria, a dreaded disease in those days. For awhile, the doctors feared for his life. But Big Six recovered and went on to win twenty-two games. It was quite a comeback.

In 1908, Matty had one of his greatest seasons. He appeared in fifty-six games, won thirty-seven, and lost just eleven. He also led the league with twelve shutouts. It was the fourth time in his career that he had won more than thirty ball games in a season. But again fate took a hand. In the final game against the Cubs, Matty pitched gallantly into the tenth. With the score tied, the Giants rallied. Shortstop Al Bidwell singled with men on first and second, and a run came home. It looked like the pennant.

As the Giants began celebrating, Cub second baseman Johnny Evers was calling for the ball. Fred Merkle, the runner on first, hadn't touched second base. He had stopped halfway between first and second when the run scored, and left the field. Technically, he was still on the base paths, and when Evers retrieved the ball and touched second, he was out!

The run didn't count. The game was ruled a tie and had to be replayed. The Giants protested, but Matty himself settled the argument.

"Merkle didn't touch second," he said sadly. But that was

his way. He had to be honest about it. In the replay, a tired Matty couldn't hold the Cubs and lost, 4–2.

Matty got into three more World Series, in 1911, 1912, and 1913. Each time, bad luck followed him. He allowed fewer than two runs a game, but won just two of seven games. He seemed jinxed. Still, he was never one to blame the other guy. He took things as they came and never complained. He was still Big Six, the top pitcher in the National League.

After winning twenty-four games in 1914, Matty suddenly began to fade. In 1915, he won just eight, and the next year, four. It was hard to believe. At the age of thirty-six, Big Six seemed finished. The years of throwing so many innings and the strain of delivering the fadeaway, with the unnatural turn of the wrist, had taken its toll on Matty's arm. The end was near and he knew it.

McGraw wanted to make it easy for his good friend and former star hurler. He knew the Cincinnati team wanted a manager, so he traded Matty. When Christy became manager of the Reds in 1917, he left a tremendous pitching record behind. He had won 373 games and lost 188. It was the most wins by a National Leaguer and, though it was later equaled by Grover Cleveland Alexander, remains the third best mark of all time, behind Cy Young and Walter Johnson.

Matty managed Cincinnati for one year. He did well. The players liked him and he was a good, patient teacher. Then the war came. Though Matty was thirty-seven years old, he enlisted in the Chemical Warfare Division and was commissioned a captain. He wasn't overseas long, but in his work near the front lines, he ran into some poison gas from the German side.

It was soon after he returned that Matty exhibited the first signs of tuberculosis. Some said it was a direct result of the gas. Others felt it had been coming all along. Matty had felt pain in his left side as early as 1916, and one of his brothers had died from the disease.

Still, it was a shock to the sports world. Big Six, a giant of a man who just a few years before was mowing down hitters for John McGraw, now lay at death's door at a sanitorium in Saranac Lake, New York.

For months, Christy was flat on his back, fighting the disease that threatened his life. Slowly, surely, he recovered. By 1922, he was in seemingly good health. He took a job as president of the Boston Braves. He was a good front office man and able administrator, but he overworked. Before long, there were signs that the disease was returning.

Perhaps he shouldn't have taken the new job. But it hurt Matty more than he thought to be out of baseball, especially in the spring, when he and Jane used to pack up and go south for training.

"I'd give anything to be going to Florida," he'd say to his wife.

"We'll go again," she assured him.

He did go south with the Braves. He was overjoyed to be back, but the strain was more than he could take. This time the tuberculosis was more than he could take, too.

Christy Mathewson died on October 7, 1925, at the age of forty-five. Baseball people were stunned. Walter Johnson, the great American League pitcher, was taking to the mound for the Senators in the World Series when he heard the news. It's said that the big hurler turned pale and tears came to his eyes. But he pulled himself together, pitched, and won the game for Matty.

A lot of people pitched for Matty in the following months.

Tributes poured in from everywhere. Even Big Six hadn't known how much he was respected and loved.

Christy Mathewson was an unlikely superstar in many ways. He was a gentleman in the days when most players were brawlers. He was well educated and refined. He never complained and took losing gracefully, never blaming anyone else for the mistakes they made. He preferred a quiet home life, and would rather play checkers, or walk in the woods, than go out on the town with the boys. He once turned down a trip around the world to remain home with his beloved wife.

But that's not how Matty is remembered. He's remembered as the man who pitched three shutouts in the 1905 World Series, as the man who won 373 games in his lifetime, as the man who threw the famous fadeaway past the best hitters of his day.

And he's remembered as Big Six, one of the two or three greatest pitchers in baseball history.

TYRUS RAYMOND COBB

The Georgia Peach

[1886–1961]

W<small>HEN YOU THINK</small> of a major league batting champion, you think of a player who hits between .320 and .350. Sometimes an even lower average will be good enough to win the bat crown, and sometimes a player will have a super year and hit even higher, maybe .360 or .365. In today's game, that's a really great average.

That makes it even more unbelievable when you look at the record of Tyrus Raymond Cobb. Here is a man who had a batting average of .367—not for one year, not for five, not for fifteen. Ty Cobb played major league baseball for twenty-four long seasons, and .367 was his lifetime average, the mark he compiled in more than eleven thousand trips to the plate.

The famed "Georgia Peach" played more games, had more at-bats, collected more hits, stole more bases, won more batting titles than any other player in history. Three times he was over the magic .400 mark. He was the American League's batting champion an even dozen times, and nine of those came in succession.

He played the game with an abandon, a will to win, a determination to succeed that has never been seen since. His career was checkered by controversy, by brawls, by accusations. Yet he kept producing the highest caliber of baseball, day in and day out, ever witnessed on a diamond.

Early in his career, Ty Cobb decided how the game of baseball should be played—all out—and he never did it any other way.

Cobb wasn't a big man, standing an even six feet tall, and weighing between 175 and 180 pounds. But he knew he'd go as far as his body would take him, and he kept himself in impeccable physical condition. He often hunted game during the off-season while wearing weighted boots to build up his legs. He continued to wear the weights during spring training, not taking them off until the first game. Then he felt as if he could walk on air, and many people swore he did.

He also played the game with his head, and was always ready to go. He never complained about having to play a ball game. In fact, there was never a single game among the 3,033 in which he played that Ty Cobb didn't give more than 100 percent.

The Georgia Peach was born on December 18, 1886, at Narrows, Georgia. His father, Professor W. H. Cobb, was a schoolmaster and state senator—a tall, striking, intelligent man who wanted his young son to follow him into a profession, preferably that of law.

For awhile, Ty leaned toward medicine, and he and the elder Cobb had long talks on the subject. Neither realized that soon both law and medicine would give way to baseball, and its hold on the youngster would be much stronger than anything else had ever been.

The game intrigued Ty from the first. When he played with his friends on the sandlots, he tried every trick to win and make himself a better ballplayer. One time he barreled into third base, knocking over one of his best friends, who dropped the ball.

"For crying out loud, Ty, was that necessary?" the boy said.

"Sorry, Mike," the young Cobb answered. "But if I didn't do that, you'd have had me out."

Soon the discussions with his father were taking a new twist.

"What do you mean, you want to play baseball," Professor Cobb roared. "You've got to go to school if you ever want to amount to anything."

"I'm not interested in school," Ty answered, just as determined. "Baseball is what I want to do and what I'm going to do. It would just be a waste of time and money for me to go to school."

The argument raged for weeks, for months. Both Cobbs were strong-willed men, and both thought they knew what was best. Both wanted to win. Ty settled the argument in 1903 when he signed a contract to play for Augusta of the Sally League. He was seventeen years old.

"So you're going to play baseball after all," said his father. "If that's what you want, I can't stop you. But let me tell you one thing. Don't come home here a failure."

The words rang clear in the youngster's head. His lips tightened. The one thing he wanted to do was make good. He had to prove to his father that he was doing the right thing, the thing he was cut out to do. He left for Augusta determined to set the baseball world on its ear.

Unfortunately, success didn't come overnight. Augusta had a tight-knit, veteran team, with a manager who was a personal friend of most of the players. When one of the regular outfielders got hurt, Ty played, and played well. But as soon as the man returned, the youngster was released.

Being cut bit hard into Ty's pride. He knew he had played well enough to stick. All he could think of was his father saying I-told-you-so. He wasn't sure what to do next when another rookie, also cut, approached him.

"Hey, Ty. I hear they got a team in Anniston [Georgia] that needs players. Why not come up with me."

Ty made his decision in a split second.

"Let's go," he said.

Anniston was a different story. The young players got a chance, and Ty was soon one of the best. It earned him another shot at Augusta in 1904. By now, the team had a new manager, a man named George Leidy, who watched young Cobb with interest.

One day Ty dropped a routine fly ball. That can happen to anyone. The only difference was that Ty was eating a bag of popcorn at the time. Leidy waited until after the game, then he took the Georgia Peach aside and really laid into him.

"I've been watching you, Ty," Leidy said. "You've got the ability to make it to the big leagues in no time. Why aren't you trying to develop your skills, instead of wasting them? Only a real busher would pull a stunt like you did today."

Leidy's tirade hit home. After that, Ty worked, and he found in the manager, an able teacher. Leidy worked with the youngster, showing him how to bunt, how to hit to all fields, and how to run the bases. Ty learned and practiced. For hours on end, he practiced.

He batted .370 at Anniston and then .326 at Augusta. The next year, 1905, he signed to play for the Detroit Tigers of the American League. Ty Cobb was about to burst onto the baseball scene for good.

About that time, there was a tragedy in the Cobb family. Ty's father was accidentally shot and killed by his mother, who mistook Mr. Cobb for a prowler. Many women in rural areas in those days kept guns for protection, and the frightened Mrs. Cobb pulled the trigger before her husband could identify himself.

It's uncertain what the impact of the tragedy was on Ty's career. Many people feel that Ty's intensity and determination to be the best resulted from the accident. He would always be trying to prove himself to his father, as he had promised, and since his father was gone, he just kept on proving himself.

At any rate, Ty batted just .240 in 41 games his rookie season. But the next year he was up to .320 in 97 games, and in 1907 he became a regular, playing in 150 games and leading the league with a .350 mark. It was the first of a record twelve batting titles Cobb would win, and started an amazing streak of nine in a row. No one player has ever dominated a league the way Ty did.

Three times, the fantastic Cobb went over the .400 mark, hitting a high of .420 in 1911. That same year he collected 248 base hits and knocked in 144 runs. And in the era of the dead ball, he did it with the benefit of just eight home runs.

Just as interesting as his amazing record is the way he did it. At the plate, Cobb was a versatile, but scientific, hitter. He choked up on the bat, and held his hands a few inches apart, allowing him to adjust to any given situation. He'd shift both hands and feet when he wanted to push the ball to left or pull it to right. Nothing was impossible for Ty when he had a bat in his hands.

On the bases, he was demon. He swiped seventy-six sacks in 1909, then set a record with ninety-six in 1915. During his great career, he pilfered 892 bases, a mark no one has come close to topping.

Perhaps, more than anything else, it was the psychological war that Ty waged on the diamond that made him so great. He was always a threat to steal, and he often came in with spikes flying. More than one time in his career he was accused of intentionally spiking an opposing player. Intentional or not, fielders thought twice when they were getting ready to slap the tag on him.

"Uncertainty plays a big part of my game," Ty once said. "The opposition doesn't know what I'm going to do next, so they can't be prepared for it. If I say I'm gonna steal, they've got to be ready for me. Every time I get a hit, they've got to be ready for me to take the extra base. They know I'm gonna do the unexpected, and it throws their game off."

Ty prided himself in his all-out approach to baseball. A writer once told him that he had just one nervous habit. Whenever Ty got on first, the writer said, he'd always kick at the bag a few times.

"Nervous habit, are you kidding me?" Cobb roared. "Heck, with the leads I used to take and the pitchers trying to pick me off, I kicked at the base to get it a few inches closer to second. And believe me, I needed every inch."

He practiced his sliding faithfully, sometimes even when his legs were a mass of bruises and welts. He mastered the hook slide and fallaway slide, where he'd catch the base with a hand or leg, while sliding past the fielder. And with most defenders bracing themselves to take the full fury of Cobb's spikes, the hook or fallaway often took them by complete surprise.

"I remember a number of times when Ty was coming my way," said a former infielder and opponent of Cobb. "I'd brace myself, figuring he was going to let me have it, and suddenly he wouldn't be there. He'd be behind me, his hand or foot on the bag and a big grin on his face."

But there were plenty of times when Cobb did things straight out. When challenged, he'd always respond.

The first sign of it came when he was at Augusta. The players didn't have showers at the stadium in those days and would take baths when they returned to their rooms. Cobb always bathed first, while his roommate, pitcher Nap Rucker, waited patiently.

One day, Rucker was knocked out of the box and returned to the room early. He took a bath. When Cobb returned and saw Rucker, he was enraged. He grumbled about Rucker's bath for hours. Finally, Nap said, "Are you trying to tell me, Ty, that no matter what happens, you want your bath first?"

Cobb looked solemn. "What I'm trying to say, Nap, is that I've got to be first—in everything."

Whenever someone challenged that first spot, he was in trouble. A catcher named Nat Criger once said that Cobb would be a "dead pigeon" if he tried to run on him. The remark got in the papers and, naturally, Ty saw it. That afternoon, he stole five bases, and one time told Criger exactly what pitches he was going to run on.

Another time, Cobb came to bat against the Yankees. A young catcher named Fred Hofmann was feeling his oats. "So this is the great Georgia Peach," he sneered.

Cobb stepped out of the box and glared down at the catcher. He didn't say a word for a second. His face turned almost beet red.

"Listen, punk," he finally exploded. "I'm getting on base now, and then I'm coming to get you."

Sure enough, Cobb singled, and promptly stole second. On

a routine grounder to the right side of the infield, he tore around third and headed for home. The throw to Hofmann had him beat, but Ty came in feet first. His spikes ripped the catcher's chest protector off, cut his right leg, and tore a shin guard away. Both went sprawling and Hofmann dropped the ball. Cobb got up first. With a half-smile, half-sneer on his face, he said, "That's right, you young squirt. That was the great Georgia Peach."

Sometimes the others fought back. Cobb is remembered for some famous brawls. One was with Buck Herzog of the Giants. It took place in Ty's hotel room and was a decidedly one-sided decision in favor of Ty. Another was with an umpire, Billy Evans, under the stands at Detroit's stadium. Ty won that one, too. In fact, witnesses say he was choking Evans when they pulled him off.

Then there was the incident in 1912, when Cobb went into the stands to fight a fan who had been riding him mercilessly for several days. Ty was suspended for that one, and his teammates walked out in sympathy. It was baseball's first strike. The next day the Tigers sent a team of semipros against the Philadelphia Athletics and were beaten, 25–2. The other players returned the next day, but Ty had to sit out his suspension.

As a batter, he showed equally little compassion. The best pitcher in the American League, at that or maybe any time, was Walter Johnson of the Senators. Johnson had a blazing fastball that could handcuff the best of hitters. But Walter was also a gentleman and nice guy, who inwardly feared he might someday kill someone with his hard one. Cobb knew of this fear.

He began crowding the plate against Johnson, actually extending his arms and elbows over the dish, banking on the fact that Johnson was too nice to throw at him. Ty was right. Johnson would try for the outside corner of the plate, and if he fell behind, he'd be forced to come in with a good pitch. By then, Cobb was ready, and, throughout the years, the technique worked well.

"I'll admit I took advantage of Walter," Cobb would say later. "I knew he wouldn't throw at me and I hit him better than anyone had a right to."

No matter what the inner and outer turmoil that always surrounded Cobb, the batting records speak for themselves. In the nine consecutive years he won the batting title, his averages were .350, .324, .377, .385, .420, .410, .390, .368, and .369. He batted a cool .371 when he lost the crown to Tris Speaker in 1916. He regained it the next three years with marks of .383, .382, and .384. It was superior hitting with amazing consistency. And Ty wasn't finished.

He batted .389 in 1921, and .401 in 1922. He didn't win the batting title either of those years, but for a player approaching thirty-six years of age, it was an amazing accomplishment. Cobb's enemies would never have the cruel pleasure of seeing him lose his batting eye. When he started to go, it was his legs that gave him the message.

The years of pounding were taking their toll. Ty couldn't run quite the way he used to, and that enraged him. He had a reputation to uphold. There was only one way he could play the game. Once his physical condition no longer permitted that, he had nothing more to give.

As late as May, 1925, when Ty was thirty-eight, he could still rise to the occasion. Some members of the St. Louis Browns had been riding him about punching the ball to left. The old determined look came over his face. Squaring off against the Browns' pitchers, Ty belted three homers, a double, and two singles, good for sixteen bases, all in a single game. The next day he hit two more homers and two long doubles. By now you'd think people would have learned not to get the Georgia Peach fired up.

For the past several years, Ty had been player-manager of the Tigers. When they released Ty the manager, they released Ty the player, too. So in 1927 he signed with Philadelphia. He was forty years old now, but wanted to show his old club they'd made a mistake. All he did was bat .357, and drive in ninety-three runs. It looked as if he'd never quit.

But he did, after the 1928 season. He still managed to hit .323, but his legs were gone and he could appear in just ninety-five games. The Georgia Peach had finally reached the end of the trail.

His batting feats are legendary; they'll always be. In 1936, he received the most votes of the five charter members of the Hall of Fame. (Ruth, Wagner, Johnson, and Mathewson were the others.) And he's still looked upon with awe today.

Cobb was a shrewd businessman as well as a ballplayer. His top salary with Detroit was $50,000, but he made some sound investments and became very wealthy. Otherwise, happiness was often difficult to find. He was divorced twice, and saw three of his children die.

Ty Cobb liked to hunt and fish, and often got together with other old ballplayers to talk about the old days. But many say he was a lonely and restless man before his death on July 17, 1961, probably never finding again the kind of challenge that baseball had put before him. To him, baseball was more than a game. It had a magnetism that brought out his physical and mental abilities to the fullest. He put his life and blood into baseball and, in doing so, gave the world a ball-player par excellence. No man will ever match his record on the diamond.

There was only one Georgia Peach. There will never be another like him.

WALTER PERRY JOHNSON
The Big Train
[1887–1946]

It WAS TWILIGHT at Washington's old Griffith Stadium. There were no lights in those days and the players scurried about, trying to finish the ball game before darkness fell. The Washington team was in the field, their big righthander tossing a few warm-up pitches, then indicating he was ready.

The first batter came to the plate. As the pitcher got ready to throw, the batter pulled out a match and quickly struck it.

"Whaddaya trying to do?" growled the umpire. "Think you'll see the ball better?"

"No, I'm not worried about that," was the rapid answer. "I just want to make sure Johnson sees me!"

The hitter wasn't crazy. On the contrary, he was smart. In the fading light of the nation's capital, he wasn't taking any chances. Because the man on the mound for the Senators was none other than Walter Johnson, the Big Train, the man who threw a baseball faster than anyone else. And there wasn't a single player in the American League in those days who relished the thought of taking a Johnson fastball in the ribs.

Nor did they relish facing the Big Train. Toiling for an annually sub-par Washington team, Walter Johnson won more games (416), tossed more shutouts (113), struck out more batters (3,508), and pitched more complete games than any pitcher in the modern era. Only Cy Young won more times than Walter, but many of his victories were in the 1890's, when the structure of the game was markedly different.

On twelve separate occasions, Sir Walter won twenty or more games, ten of those years coming in succession. Yet it was always a struggle, because no one ever knew if the lowly Senators would score as much as a single run.

"I guess the only time Walter could be sure of a win was when he tossed a shutout," said one veteran reporter. "That's probably why he threw so many of them."

There's plenty of truth in that statement. Statistics show that the Big Train was involved in sixty-four 1–0 decisions during his career. He won thirty-eight of them; the rest were heartbreaking defeats. And when he wasn't tossing shutouts, he was throwing some pretty low-hit games. Walter had just a single no-hitter to his credit, but in 1913 alone he hurled five one-hitters, a record that's sure to stand for a good long time.

Throughout the years, many baseball people have come along to challenge Johnson's standing as the fastest pitcher ever.

"Grove's faster," they said of the Philadelphia left-hander.

"Feller throws harder than Johnson," was the cry when Rapid Robert emerged on the Cleveland scene.

There has been a succession of pretenders since, men such as Herb Score, Sandy Koufax, Nolan Ryan, and Vida Blue. It's really impossible to compare these mound aces of different eras. There weren't clocking devices in Johnson's day, and many pitchers will cut loose with a little extra when they know it's for clocking. They certainly don't throw the same kind of pitch they'd throw at a hitter in a tight situation.

But perhaps a better barometer comparing Johnson with the others is this. Almost every other fastballer down through the years has learned to use another pitch to advantage; either a curve, slider, or change-up. That way, he can keep the hitters off balance, set up his fastball, and keep the batters guessing in different situations.

Not the Big Train. Walter was a one-pitch pitcher, that's all. A youngster coming up today with just one pitch would be sent back to the minors for seasoning and instruction. But for almost two decades, batters knew what to expect from Johnson. He'd wind up facing straight at the batter, hands directly in front of his face. The right arm would sweep back until the ball appeared on the other side of his body. Then he'd uncork in a sweeping, sidearm motion, considered the most natural and least-straining way to throw a baseball.

WHOOOSH. The ball would smack into the catcher's mitt in a split second. Every time. Walter was a fastball pitcher and a fastball pitcher only. It wasn't until late in his career that he even attempted to develop a curve, and, at most, it was a weak one. The fastball sustained him to the last. It was the only pitch he threw, but it was enough.

There's another Johnson story that bears retelling here, because it also serves to indicate the blazing speed of Walter Johnson's fastball. It was another of those twilight games in Washington, and the Senators were trying to finish it in a hurry. Johnson had two strikes on the hitter when he and catcher Gabby Street decided to pull a fast one of their own.

The Big Train pumped and delivered. Only he held the ball in his glove. An instant later, Street slammed his bare fist into the mitt. The plate umpire didn't hesitate.

"Strike three!" he bellowed.

The batter didn't argue. He just turned around and left the plate. That's how fast Walter Johnson threw the baseball. It didn't have to be seen to be believed, and as this story points out, sometimes it wasn't.

Johnson's fastball in the hands of a hell-for-leather competitor like Ty Cobb or Rogers Hornsby would have been considered a lethal weapon. But the Train, as menacing as he looked on the mound, was probably one of the most even-tempered, low-keyed performers ever to play in the Bigs.

"Sometimes this thing really scares me," he once said, referring to his fastball. "I'm afraid if I hit someone with it, I'll kill him."

It was a genuine concern to gentleman Walter. They say he only threw one brush-back pitch in his life, at Frank (Home Run) Baker, when his teammates urged him to draw some revenge after a couple of Senators had been plinked by his mound rival.

Johnson's fast one whistled in at Baker's side and the ballplayer dropped out of the way just in time. Walter's legs began quivering and he turned sheet-white.

"Never again," he said later. "I couldn't forgive myself if I ever injured a man intentionally."

Ty Cobb knew about Johnson's good nature, crowding the plate and daring Walter to move him back. But the Big Train would shoot for the outside corner, and if he didn't hit it, he'd be forced to come in with a little less than his hard one. Cobb was ready, and the technique got him a few more hits off Walter than he normally would have made. Walter knew what Ty was doing, yet he never complained or became angered. He just tried to cope with the situation as best he could.

Walter Perry Johnson was born on November 6, 1887, at Humboldt, Kansas, in the heart of farm country. His parents, Frank and Minnie Johnson, were farmers whose ancestors had come west from Pennsylvania in the early days when the wagon trains carried people across country in their search for new lives.

Taking a cue from their migrating ancestors, the Johnsons went to California in 1901, at a time when many farmers gave up poor lands to search for oil in the Far West.

There was no oil for the Johnsons, but they went into the business of supplying horses and mules to oilmen who needed work animals to pull equipment. It provided a livable income and also got young Walter working so hard that he quickly became a strapping youngster, with broad shoulders and muscular arms. When he was about thirteen, he was already the star catcher for a local team, the Oil Field Juniors. The reason he caught was that no player could catch him. He was already too fast.

By 1907, Walter was pitching for the Weiser Telephone Company team. When there was no game, he dug post holes, but was considered a professional ballplayer nevertheless. A traveling salesman took one look at the speedballing youngster and telegrammed his friend, Washington Senators' Manager Joe Cantillon, to get someone out to look at the big righty.

Cantillon was skeptical, but he had an injured catcher, Cliff Blankenship, hanging around, so he told him to hop a train and take a look at the youngster. Blankenship saw Walter pitch and lose a twelve-inning game 1–0, but he lost on errors and was obviously a pitcher with a future.

Blankenship whipped out a one hundred dollar bill.

"Here's a bonus right now, kid," he said after the game.

"There's $350 more a month waiting for you if you join the Senators."

Johnson's only question was one that most of the poor boys in those days asked.

"What about traveling expenses?" he said.

When Blankenship laughed and told him not to worry, Walter agreed. A contract was drawn up on the first old piece of paper they found. Walter and his father both signed it, and the younger Johnson packed off to Washington.

It wasn't until Walter signed with Washington that he learned he wasn't pitching in total obscurity after all. Both Seattle (a minor league team) and the Pittsburgh Pirates of the National League had scouts traveling to see him pitch at that very moment. Pittsburgh, in fact, had received a tip about Walter earlier and ignored it. Fortunately for Washington, the Senators acted when they got their tip.

Walter's big league debut came in August of that year. He pitched well against the Detroit Tigers, but cagey old Ty Cobb took advantage of the raw rookie with two bunts, the second of which brought home the deciding run, and Johnson was a 3-2 loser.

In fourteen games that first year, Walter finished with a 5-9 record. The next year he was 14-14, but in 1909, his mark was just 13-25. Though he hadn't quite matured as a pitcher, Johnson was already experiencing the shoddy support and light hitting from his Senator teammates that would continue for almost his entire career.

For years, there was an old maxim in the streets of Capitol Hill—"Washington: first in war, first in peace, and last in the American League." How true, and it was the kind-hearted Walter's fate to pitch uncomplainingly with the Senators for twenty-one years.

But by 1910, it didn't matter what kind of support he got. Walter emerged as a superpitcher. Sportswriter Grantland Rice was the man who gave Walter his nickname, equating Johnson's fastball with the fastest mode of transportation at that time, the train. Hence, the Big Train. And the Big Train won a big twenty-five games that season, losing seventeen.

It's probably safe to say that at least five of Walter's losses each year could be attributed directly to the play of his teammates. His record with a stronger team would have been even more amazing.

Walter started forty-five games that year, tossed eight shutouts, and struck out 313 batters. One of the newspapers covering the Senators then had this to say about the big pitcher:

"A bolt of greased lightning has burst onto the Washington scene. His name is Walter P. Johnson and he throws a baseball harder than anyone can remember. This big fastballer won 25 games last year, and would have won more had the Senators not played their usual sub-par baseball. But Johnson seems above and oblivious to the play of his teammates. He stands out there, firing his fastball, time and again, and the hitters wave hopelessly at the air, trying to connect."

The Big Train was, indeed, a formidable-looking figure on the mound. He stood 6'1" and weighed a solid 200 pounds. But with so much of the weight concentrated in his shoulders and arms, he looked a lot bigger. He had a strong face, with high cheekbones and a square jaw. His almost perfect nose, sandy hair, and blue eyes made him look more like a leading man than an athlete. Someone once said that Johnson looked like an Adonis, a kind of handsome god on the mound, sent to pitch by some divine power.

But he was no god. There were too many tough losses for

that. Fortunately, the wins came, too. He duplicated his twenty-five victories in 1911, then won thirty-two in 1912, and compiled a fantastic 36–7 mark in 1913.

It was one of the greatest seasons ever compiled by a major league pitcher. Walter started 48 games, pitched 346 innings, hurled 12 shutouts, set records with five one-hitters and 56 straight scoreless innings. He fanned 243 batters and walked just 38. His earned-run average per nine-inning game was just 1.14, a mark topped only by present day pitcher Bob Gibson of the Cards. A few years ago, Gibson's ERA was 1.12, but he didn't pitch nearly as often as Walter.

That was a banner year for Walter in more ways than one. He also met his future wife, the daughter of a Nevada congressman, Hazel Lee Roberts. She was a big baseball fan and loved coming out to watch Walter pitch. It didn't take long for the two to fall in love and they were married the following June, in 1914.

That year, Walter's record slipped a bit, to 28–18. He still had ten shutouts and an earned run average of 1.72, indicating that many of his losses were the result of the usual poor support and weak hitting from his teammates. But despite the increase in losses, the Big Train had a three-year-mark of 96–37, and with a wife and soon-to-be family, he felt he should be better paid for his efforts.

At that time, Walter was earning some $12,000 per year, not a bad sum for those days. But he was a superpitcher with a terrible team, and one of the main reasons the Senators drew well at the gate. Whenever the Big Train was scheduled to take the mound, several thousand more fans would jam into the old ballpark.

Clark Griffith, the boss of the Senators, said he didn't think Walter was worth more money.

"Heck, Walter," said Griffith in one of the all-time twists of logic, "you didn't have that good a year. You only won twenty-eight games."

But the Big Train, who hated squabbling, had a trump card. There was a new league forming then, the Federal League, and the Feds were trying to corner the market on all the good ballplayers they could afford. They offered Walter $16,000 plus another $10,000 as a bonus. Walter demanded that the Senators meet the price.

Faced with the prospect of losing his number one star, Griffith came up with the $16,000, but he still needed the other ten grand. He got it in a strange way. He contacted Charles Comiskey, a owner of the Chicago White Sox, and asked him for the money.

"What, are you nuts!" exclaimed Comiskey.

"No, I'm not," Griffith said calmly. "How would you like Walter Johnson to be pitching for the Chicago Club in the Federal League? They're trying to get him, and if they do, he'll take half your customers away."

Comiskey thought it over, saw the reasoning, and delivered the goods. Johnson had his money and remained with the Senators.

The Big Train continued to win, and to be victimized by the poor play of his teammates. He won twenty-seven, twenty-five, twenty-three, twenty-three, and twenty over the next five years. So bad were the rest of the Senators that Walter was a twenty-game loser, 25–20, in 1916, despite having an earned-run average of 1.89, a highly unlikely baseball situation. A lesser man might have raved incessantly, demanding to be traded. Not Johnson. He took his fate like a gentleman, pitching the best he could and urging his teammates on.

Then in 1920, the 33-year-old Big Train came up with the first sore arm of his career. It kept him out of action for part of the season, and he finished with an 8–10 record. The only bright spot was a no-hitter. Typically, the one base runner reached the sack on an error, or Walter would have had a perfect game.

Johnson wasn't quite the same pitcher the next three seasons. His record was 17–14, 15–16, and 17–12. He was thirty-six years old when the 1924 season opened, and many people were saying that the old man was about washed up. His fast one wasn't quite as fast, and he never developed an effective curve to go with the blazer. The ironic part of it was that the Senators finally had a respectable team.

"If we had the old Johnson, we'd have a shot at the pennant," said a Washington coach.

"The old man might fool a few people," said another.

Johnson did fool a lot of people. Used wisely by his manager, Bucky Harris, the Big Train started just 38 games, but led the team with a mark of 23–7. Included were 6 shutouts and 158 strikeouts. And as the man said, with the old Johnson, the Senators finally won a pennant.

The sentiment was with Johnson. People had lamented for years because Walter had never been in a series. Now, with Washington facing the powerful New York Giants, he'd finally have his chance to fill a long-time ambition—winning a World Series game. It was his eighteenth season in the majors.

As expected, the Big Train was the opening-game pitcher for the Senators. Turning back the clock, Walter was superb, firing his fastball past the bewildered Giant hitters in the early innings. They thought the old man would be a soft touch. He started tiring in the latter innings, but at the end of nine, the score was knotted at 2–2. Johnson pitched into the twelfth. It wasn't unusual to see his teammates handcuffed. Then in the twelfth, the aging arm ran out of steam, and the Giants pushed across two runs. Washington got one back, but lost the game, 4–3.

Walter Johnson was the loser. He had fanned twelve Jints, but gave up fourteen hits. It was a courageous performance and a heartbreaking defeat. Washington then came on to win two of the next three games to tie the Series at two games each.

In the fifth game, it was the Train again. This time he wasn't as sharp, giving up three runs in the eighth and eventually losing, 6–2.

The Senators fought back and won the sixth game, and the Series went to a seventh and deciding game.

The Giants held an early 3–1 lead, but the Senators tied it up in the eighth. That's when Manager Harris brought in a new pitcher. It was Walter Johnson. The old man would have another chance for a win.

With the Series on the line, Walter called on every bit of power his aging arm could muster. For four innings, the Big Train held the Giants. Then in the last of the twelfth, Lady Luck finally smiled on him. Earl McNeely hit a bad hop grounder to score Muddy Ruel with the winning run. The Senators were world champs and Johnson had won the deciding game.

"If any player on the field deserved victory, it was Walter Johnson," the papers said the next day. "The famed Big Train waited 18 years to get into the World Series, pitched well, but lost two games. Given a third chance, the great man held the Giants for four innings and destiny prevailed. A pitcher as good as Walter Johnson has been over the years deserves to be a world champion."

The next season, Walter was good again. He won twenty games (20–7) for the twelfth and last time in his career, and the Senators won the pennant again. This time Walter didn't have to wait. He won the first game from the Pittsburgh Pirates, 4–1, then shut out the Pirates, 4–0, on six hits in game four. But the Pirates stormed back to tie the Series at three games each.

Then it was Johnson again in the seventh game. The field in Pittsburgh was soaked by an all-day rain, and it was still coming down when Walter took to the mound. His teammates gave him a lead, 4–0, but he couldn't hold it. The Pirates chipped away. The mound was wet and slippery, and the Train couldn't get his footing. Two runs in the seventh and three in the eighth settled the issue. The Pirates won it, 9–7, and were world champs.

Johnson had pitched the entire game. He had been hit hard, but only six of the nine runs were earned. Manager Harris was heavily criticized for sticking with the old man for so long, but he defended his choice vehemently.

"There's no man in the world I'd rather have on the mound than Walter Johnson," he said. "When you're in a big game, you go with your best, and Walter's the best there is."

Whether Harris was right or wrong, it was obviously getting close to the end. The next year Walter was 15–16, with a high earned-run average of 3.61. The next year he broke a leg, missed part of the season, and had a 5–6 mark. After twenty-one years in the majors, the big guy called it quits.

Walter managed at Newark for a year, then replaced Harris as Senators' manager in 1929. But tragedy struck. Walter's wife died in 1930, and the Train had to raise five children.

Being away from home became more difficult for him. He became surly and aloof. There were other things on his mind. After four years at Washington, he went over to Cleveland for a year, then dropped out of baseball.

His last years were spent on a large farm in Maryland, near his old stomping grounds at Washington. He raised cattle, loved to hunt and spend time with his dogs. An original member of the Hall of Fame since 1936, Walter had many friends and admirers, and often attended baseball functions and reunions.

Then, in 1946, Walter was struck down by a brain tumor. It grew worse. On December 10, the Big Train died quietly on his Maryland farm. He was just fifty-nine years old.

Johnson legends grow with the years. He's often compared with hard-throwing youngsters and his records placed alongside that of other greats, like Mathewson, Alexander, and Cy Young. Whether he's ranked on top or not, the Big Train was as good as they come.

His catcher, Gabby Street, once decided to try a stunt that had never been done before. He became the first man ever to catch a ball dropped from the Washington monument. Street circled around and caught the ball, the impact making him stagger and almost fall. It was hailed as a great accomplishment by those who thought it couldn't be done.

"Heck, it was easy," Street claimed later. "You forget, I've been catching Walter Johnson's fastball for years now."

TRIS SPEAKER
The Grey Eagle

[1888–1958]

FOR MANY YEARS, whenever someone was asked to name the three best outfielders who ever played the game of baseball, the answer went very much like this:

"Let's see, I'll put Cobb in left, Ruth in right, and . . . Speaker in center."

The decision was always final. Cobb, Ruth, Speaker. Ruth, Cobb, Speaker. The first two names, widely known and respected, were interchangeable. The third, that of Tristram Speaker, was always mentioned last, but remained part of the trio.

In recent years, though with younger fans making the choice, the question is answered somewhat differently. The first two names still prevail. But in the third spot there have been changes. Now the third outfielder cited may be Joe DiMaggio, or Willie Mays, or Henry Aaron. Speaker is mentioned with less and less frequency as the years pass.

The point is this. Babe Ruth and Ty Cobb became legends in their own time. Tris Speaker didn't. He always played in shadows. Now, as the years go by, Speaker seems on the brink of becoming a forgotten man, a legend that never was, a ballplayer whose feats and skills are no longer remembered.

Just who was this man they called the Grey Eagle? Let's look at the record. Tris Speaker played major league baseball for twenty-two years. He had a lifetime batting average of .344. Only Ty Cobb, Rogers Hornsby, Joe Jackson, and Lefty O'Doul have done better. In that time he stroked out 793 doubles. No one in history has topped that. He also collected 3,515 hits, trailing only Cobb and Stan Musial in that department. He holds the major league record for assists by an outfielder in a season, thirty-five, and he did that twice. He has the most lifetime putouts of any outfielder, the most assists, the most chances accepted. He was a batting champion, a Most Valuable Player, a playing manager. And he was named to the Hall of Fame in 1937, just a year after it came into existence.

A direct comparison with the man who most often upstages him now, DiMaggio, shows the following results. Speaker played nine more seasons than Joe, made 1,301 more hits, had 404 more doubles, 93 more triples, scored 491 more runs, and stole 403 more bases. His lifetime batting average was nineteen points higher. The only place Joltin' Joe has an advantage is in home runs, 361 to 115, but Speaker played in the era of the dead ball.

Joe DiMaggio was a great ballplayer. No one can deny that. He was recently voted the Greatest Living Ballplayer of any era. You can't argue with Joe's credentials. But where does that leave Tris Speaker? Without question, very close to the head of the class.

Tristram Speaker was a brash, outgoing player who wasn't afraid to speak up to teammates, managers, or owners. He knew he could back his boasts with his ability. He always knew where he was going, and if he were still on the scene today he'd probably have a thing or two to say about some of

the modern ballplayers who are pushing him out of the limelight.

The Speaker saga began on April 4, 1888, at Hubbard
City, Texas. Tristram was born into a large family, and when
he was just ten, his father died. That left young Tris free to
do pretty much as he pleased. He was close to his mother,
but she didn't really have time to ride herd on her large
brood.

Tris had time to do plenty of riding, though. He learned
about horses early, and was soon tackling the wildest and
most high-spirited ones he could find. Half the time he didn't
bother to use a saddle or bridle.

But his recklessness finally caught up to him. One day,
while trying a little bronco busting, he was thrown and suffered a broken right arm. It may have been a blessing in dis-
guise. Because he couldn't wait for the arm to heal, Tris
began throwing a baseball left-handed, and batting the same
way. Even after the arm healed, he remained a southpaw.

He was a star right through high school, playing both football and baseball. Then, in 1905, he enrolled at Fort Worth
Polytechnic Institute, forgot about football, and concentrated
on the diamond game. He pitched and played the outfield,
and hit the ball all over the lot.

During his sophomore year at Poly, he often played for a
local semipro team in nearby Corsicana. One afternoon, a
man named Doak Roberts sat in the stands watching them
play. He owned the Cleburne team of the North Texas
League, and had come out to look at one of the local team's
outfielders. Tris was pitching that day and it didn't take long
for Roberts to spot the young Texan.

Aside from some nifty hurling, Tris belted two solid home

runs and was obviously the outstanding player on the field. Roberts asked him if he'd like to play proball with Cleburne.

Tris jumped at the chance, took his train fare from Roberts, and hopped a freight down to Waco, where he sought out the Cleburne manager, Barney Shelton. The problem was that he woke Shelton in the wee hours of the morning and immediately got on the wrong side of the manager.

The next day he worked out with the team, pitched batting practice, and took his turn in the cage, hitting sharp line drives to all fields. He was ready to towel off and watch the game when Shelton told him to get ready to pitch.

"Warm up, Speaker," the manager said.

"Are you kidding?" bellowed Tris. "I've been out here for an hour already. I'm red hot!"

Tris pitched, all right. He nursed a 2–1 lead into the ninth. Then, with two men on, the ball was hit to Manager Shelton, who was playing first base. There was a close play at the bag, and Shelton started to argue, holding the ball while the tying and winning runs crossed the plate.

The young pitcher exploded. He cursed out the manager, and when some of the players told him to calm down, he challenged any of them to fight him. When owner Roberts returned that night, he found the team in a turmoil.

"What happened?" he asked.

"That Speaker kid you sent down here," one of the players said, "he's crazy."

Roberts found Speaker and got his side of the story, which was the only side. Tris didn't lie. He admitted what he had done. Roberts talked to the youngster for a long time, then offered him a contract for $50.00 a month, but made him promise to apologize to Shelton.

Tris said he was sorry, but the manager, looking for revenge, pitched him again the next day. This time even Tris couldn't make it. He gave up twenty-two runs before Shelton gleefully removed him. But the day after, the Cleburne rightfielder was hurt. Tris approached his manager with a sneer.

"You need another rightfielder," he said. "Well, put me out there. I'm the best rightfielder in the league."

Shelton sneered right back, but he needed an outfielder and decided to let the kid take his lumps. There were no lumps to be had. One look at Tris patrolling the outfield convinced him. That's where Tris stayed. When the season ended, Tris had played in eighty-four games and had a mediocre .268 average. But the potential was there. With the team transferred to the Houston area in 1907, Tris played the full schedule and batted .314.

For the next two seasons, the young Texan played a game of musical teams in a strange case of a superplayer trying to get to the majors.

The success story started when Roberts, always very high on the youngster, made a deal with the St. Louis Browns. He'd wire the Browns when he thought Speaker was ready and they'd buy his contract. Roberts sent his wire, all right, but got no answer. So he sent another. Still no reply.

Finally, he gave up and contacted the Boston Red Sox. They bought the outfielder's contract for $800. Tris was called up at the end of the season, but the Sox didn't think he showed enough for a contract.

An angered Speaker picked up and went to the Giants' training camp at Marlin, Texas, and brazenly approached the great John McGraw.

"Need an outfielder?" he said. "If you do, I'm the guy you're looking for."

"Sorry, kid," said Little Napoleon. "We're full up. Besides, I don't go around signing kids I never heard of."

Undaunted, Tris paid his own way back to the Red Sox camp in Arkansas and finally succeeded in talking himself into a contract. But the Sox left him behind, bequeathing him to the Little Rock club instead of the rent money they owed. Tired of double-dealing with everyone, Tris settled down and let his bat do the talking. He swatted a blazing .350 at Little Rock, and suddenly the offers poured in, from the Senators, the Pirates, the Giants. But the Little Rock manager felt he was obligated to the Red Sox and sold Tris to Boston late in the 1908 season. Speaker was finally in the majors to stay.

His first full season, 1909, he batted .309, and drove in seventy-nine runs. The next year he shot up to .340, then .327, .383, .365. He was an established star, but still hadn't won a batting title. Another young ballplayer named Cobb was in the midst of nine in a row. Speaker was to play his entire career in the shadow of the great Georgia Peach.

But there was one area in which Spoke excelled. That was playing the outfield. Cobb had an average arm; Ruth wasn't that fast. But Speaker could do it all. It's doubtful that there ever has been a centerfielder like him. Even the two usually put in the same class with the Grey Eagle—DiMaggio and Mays—had only a third as many assists as Speaker was to compile in his lifetime.

Tris played an unusually shallow centerfield. He could do it more easily in the day of the dead ball, as there were fewer long drives then. And Spoke had his own philosophy about it.

"There's so much more activity in front of you than behind you," he said. "I'd rather be in position to come in and grab the short ones and the cheap ones, than worry about a long one getting away. I just feel I'm more valuable to the team playing shallow."

Spoke knew the hitters and knew how to go back on a ball. So even though he played shallow, not many were belted over his head. And some of the things he did from his centerfield position are all but unheard of today.

On several occasions he was credited with unassisted double plays by grabbing low liners on the dead run and continuing on to second base to trap a returning baserunner. He also figured in standard double plays by taking a throw from the second baseman and relaying on to first. This wasn't a routine play, but he did it more than once.

He also helped his club cover on some sacrifice plays, by running in and taking second, allowing the shortstop to cover third. Things like this just aren't done anymore. He could go back on a ball to his right or left with equal ease, and he possessed a strong, accurate throwing arm that cut down runners at a record-setting pace.

The Red Sox won a pennant in 1912, the year Tris hit .383 and drove in ninety-eight runs. In the World Series, the Sox faced the powerful New York Giants and their ace righthander, Christy Mathewson. It was a close, exciting series all the way. It went down to the seventh game. With Matty on the mound, the Giants broke a 1–1 tie in the tenth and were three outs away from winning.

Boston began to rally. A Fred Snodgrass error helped get a man on base. After a walk, Tris stepped up. Matty tried to slip one by on the inside corner, and Tris lofted a foul pop down the first base line. The first baseman, catcher, and Matty himself all went for the ball. Any one of them could have caught it, but they got their signals crossed and let it drop.

Tris smiled. A hitter like Spoke doesn't blow a second chance. On the next pitch he lined a single to right, scoring the tying run. When the next batter hit a long, sacrifice fly, the Red Sox were world champions.

Three years later, Tris's career at Boston came to an abrupt end. It was after the 1915 season. An attempt at a third major league, the Federal League, had just failed, and many of the owners were cutting salaries. The Red Sox trimmed Tris's pay from $18,000 to $9,000. The Eagle snorted, and said he wouldn't play unless he received at least $15,000.

The stalemate continued into the 1916 exhibition season. Just when Tris thought the Red Sox were about to meet his price, he got a phone call from Bob McRoy, general manager of the Cleveland Indians.

"Ever think about playing in Cleveland?" McRoy asked. Speaker was puzzled.

"Not really," he answered, a little annoyed at the whole affair. "You don't have much of a ballclub over there, and I don't really like your town." It was the old Speaker brashness.

"I'm sorry you feel that way," McRoy said. "We've just traded with the Red Sox for you."

Tris was stunned. He hadn't really thought about leaving the Sox. At first, he said he wouldn't go. Then he found out the deal had been signed. He balked again, telling the Red Sox he'd go only if he received $10,000 of the purchase price. The Sox didn't want everything to fall through, so they consented. Once again, the Grey Eagle had spoken his piece, and he'd come out on top.

He also came out on top at Cleveland. Once he was settled, he proceeded to tear apart the American League with his bat. Determined to show the Red Sox they had made a mistake, Spoke batted .386 and won his first and only American League batting title.

When asked how it felt to win the bat crown after so many years of top-flight hitting, Spoke answered with a grin.

"I figured Ty was getting bored winning all those titles. A little change might do him some good."

Tris was referring to the nine straight bat crowns won by the Georgia Peach. And he was right. After Speaker won his, Ty went on to win three more. It hadn't been easy for the Grey Eagle to play second fiddle all those years. It wasn't part of his nature. But he respected Cobb's talents and figured it was best to make a joke out of it.

From that point, Tris went about his business of making a new home in Cleveland. It didn't take him long. His smooth style in the field, potent bat, and flamboyant personality quickly endeared him to a new set of fans. When the team began searching for a new manager midway through the 1919 season, they stopped at centerfield. Tris Speaker became playing manager of the Cleveland Indians.

In undertaking his new responsibilities, the Grey Eagle's batting average dipped below .300 to .296 for the first time since his rookie season. But he more than made up for it the next year, managing and batting the Indians to the American League pennant. Spoke garnered 214 hits, batted .388, and drove home 107 runs. He was so popular he could have been elected mayor if he had so chosen.

Tris went on to bat .320 in the Series, as the Indians toppled the Brooklyn Dodgers in seven games. He was a hero and superstar throughout the baseball world.

"Never has a player-manager put together as successful a season as Tris Speaker," read the text of one newspaper story. "Not only did the Grey Eagle make a .388 batting average and drive in more than 100 runs, but he managed with the guile of a Mack or a McGraw. Throughout the year, baseball people criticized his platooning, his handling of players, and his pitching rotation. But Spoke proved them all wrong, as he had time and again throughout his great career."

And the career continued, Tris performing his dual role with relative ease. As a thirty-seven year old in 1925, Tris married the former Frances Cudahy of Buffalo, and celebrated by batting a career high of .389. P.S.—It wasn't good enough for a batting title. Again.

Tris might have entertained ideas about staying on as manager after his playing days ended, but that notion was dispelled after the 1926 season. A little-known player named Hubert (Dutch) Leonard came up with a story saying that Speaker and Ty Cobb had conspired to throw a late-season game several years before. Both stars denied the charge and were eventually cleared by Commissioner Kenesaw Landis.

But the accusation was enough. Both Tris and Cobb, who was player-manager at Detroit, were eased out of their jobs. Baseball was still nervous from the Black Sox Scandal of 1919, and didn't want the whispers going around.

Spoke then signed with Washington and batted .327 for the 1927 season, playing in 141 games. The next year, he moved over to Philadelphia, where he and Cobb finished their careers as teammates.

It was a time of mixed emotions for the two old superstars and rivals. They both knew they were near the end of the line, and that was sad. But as teammates, they could spend the year enjoying the game they loved so much and sharing memories of two great careers.

Tris played in just sixty-four games that year, his forty-year-old legs unable to go at full speed. He batted .267 and then decided to retire.

The next year, Spoke was managing at Newark in the International League. He decided to play part time, just to show the younger guys how to do it. Amazingly, he still had enough left to bat .355 in 138 trips to the plate. He did the same thing in 1930, this time coming up only thirty-one times, but still managing thirteen hits for a .419 clip. The Grey Eagle could always handle the bat.

After that, Spoke drifted to other fields. He was a broadcaster for awhile, and was involved in several other baseball-related ventures. He later turned to the wholesale liquor business and also worked with a Detroit steel company. Always a good businessman, Spoke did well, and lived comfortably in his later life.

He came back to baseball once more, as a special coach with the Indians in 1947. They wanted him to help convert Larry Doby, the American League's first black player, from a second baseman to a centerfielder. They called in the best man for the job.

Tris Speaker died of a heart attack on December 8, 1958, while visiting friends in his native Texas. He was seventy years old.

Years have passed since his death, and his name is no longer a household word as it was once. But ask any of those who saw him. They'll tell you just how good Tris Speaker was. There was only one Grey Eagle, and he'll always be among the greatest ever to grace the national pastime.

GEORGE HERMAN RUTH

The Babe

[1895–1948]

H<small>E DIDN'T LOOK</small> much like a ballplayer, especially in his later years. He had a round, cherubic face with a broad nose, a big belly, and spindly legs. His arms didn't bulge with muscle, and he walked with an odd, pigeon-toed gait. But when he stood at home plate, bat in hand, and looked out menacingly at the pitcher, every one of his rivals quaked with fear.

For Babe Ruth could hit a baseball like no man before or since. When the Babe laced into one, it traveled very high and very far, and always landed deep in the distant seats. Fans cheered wildly as the rotund slugger trotted around the bases, a grin on his mischievous face, another home run logged into the record book.

People paid to see the Babe paste one. It was worth more than the price of admission to them. He was their guy, whether they rooted for the New York Yankees or not. George Herman Ruth was the man most responsible for rescuing baseball from its darkest hour and bringing it back to prominence as the national pastime for a sports-crazy generation in the 1920's.

Although the big Babe was the greatest slugger the game has ever known, that wasn't the limit of his baseball talents.

Ruth could do it all. He started as a pitcher with the Boston Red Sox and quickly became a two-time, twenty-game winner, setting some records that still stand.

When his hitting dictated a switch to the outfield, he soon showed he could handle his position with the best of them. He was even an outstanding base runner. Observers say that the Babe never threw to a wrong base, never made a mental error on the diamond. He didn't have to think about what he was doing. It all came naturally. In fact, the Babe was probably the most natural baseball player who ever lived.

Off the field, the great Bambino was also in a class by himself. He was a fun-loving, free-spending personage, who loved to eat, drink, and be merry. And he loved kids, becoming a friend and idol to countless numbers during his lifetime. His off-field exploits would come back and haunt him someday, but during the early days of his career, the Babe was having a ball.

Always, he remained serious about his baseball. And when he finally quit, Babe Ruth had hit more home runs and had driven in more runs than any man in the history of the game. His lifetime batting average was a sensational .342, and the scope of his baseball achievements endless.

But the Babe wasn't always on top. He had his share of hardships, right from the time he was a little boy.

George Herman Ruth was born in Baltimore, Maryland, on February 6, 1895. His father owned a saloon in that city and had to work very hard to earn a living. Young George began roaming the streets early, and it wasn't long before he was getting into trouble.

"I was a bum when I was a kid," he said regretfully, years later. "I even used to steal from my own parents."

And young George was quickly picking up some other bad habits. He chewed tobacco by the time he was seven and drank whiskey before he was ten. Both his parents were very worried. They couldn't keep him off the streets and out of trouble. Finally, they decided to send him to St. Mary's Industrial School for Boys.

The school housed orphans and delinquent youngsters. George was to spend much of his time there until he joined the Baltimore Orioles of the International League in 1914.

If it weren't for his stay at St. Mary's, George Herman Ruth might never have played baseball. But, fortunately, he met a man there who saw the seeds of his great skills, and also believed in the young boy as a human being.

The man was Brother Matthias, one of the Xaverians who ran the school. Brother Matthias was six and a half feet tall, and weighed 250 pounds. This mountain of a man was also gentle and kind. He befriended the lonely boy and began to teach him some very important things, such as reading and writing, and the difference between right and wrong. But he also taught him how to play baseball.

"I always felt I could hit the ball, even the first time I held a bat," Babe Ruth once said. "But Brother Matthias taught me some other things. He made me a pitcher and showed me how to field. He really knew the game of baseball and he loved it."

For almost a dozen years, Brother Matthias worked with George. But it was another Xaverian, Brother Gilbert, who finally got the boy his big break. Brother Gilbert was a friend of Jack Dunn, who owned the Orioles of the International League. When Dunn learned of the youngster's great talents from Brother Gilbert, he signed papers with the state making him responsible for George until the boy turned twenty-one.

George was about to become a professional ballplayer.

When he left St. Mary's for the last time on February 27, 1914, Brother Matthias was at the front gate. He shook the boy's hand and said quietly, "You'll make it, George."

With five dollars in his pocket, young George rode a train to Fayetteville, North Carolina, to join the Orioles in spring training. It was here that George Herman acquired a new name. On his first day of practice, he was trailing along after Jack Dunn, club owner, when someone remarked, "Here comes Jack with his newest babe."

In the first intra-squad game, the Babe hit a mammoth homer. But he was a pitcher, and everyone considered it something of a fluke.

His pitching surely wasn't a fluke. Firing his fastball from the left side, the Babe was an instant success. Within three months, his contract was purchased by the Boston Red Sox and he was shipped to Providence, also in the International League. He promptly pitched the minor league club to the pennant and was the best pitcher in the league, winning twenty-two games and losing just nine.

In 1915, the Babe joined the Red Sox. He was a big leaguer now, and a big leaguer to stay. There was no way he could be kept in the minors any longer.

With Ruth winning eighteen games in 1915, and twenty-three in each of the next two years, the Red Sox became the best team in baseball, winning a pair of World Series. In fact, the Babe was a star in the fall classic, winning three games without a loss and setting a record of 29⅔ consecutive scoreless innings, a mark that stood for many, many years.

But something else happened in 1915 that would eventually have a great effect on the Babe's career. The Sox were playing the Yankees early in the season and Babe came up to hit against a pitcher named Jack Warhop. Pitchers are usually poor hitters, and Warhop didn't take the big youngster too seriously. Neither did his Yankee teammates, and they gave the big guy the business.

Put the big oaf in your pocket, Jack.

Blow it by the bum!

Show him how a real pitcher throws.

Babe stood in the batter's box facing the Yankee hurler. The catcalls didn't bother him. He was relaxed, feet planted solidly and held close together. Warhop threw a fastball and the Babe swung. His timing was perfect. The ball jumped off the bat as if it had been shot from a cannon. It kept going higher and higher. When it finally came down, it landed deep in the rightfield seats.

Warhop and the rest of the Yankees were astonished. They didn't believe the big kid could hit a ball that far. It was the day of the dead ball, and not many homers were hit at all. Pitchers almost never hit one.

But the Babe was no ordinary pitcher. That home run was just his first. Before he finished, there would be some seven hundred more of them.

While Ruth was compiling his fine pitching record, Sox manager Ed Barrow couldn't help notice the way Babe hit the ball. For two years he played with an idea over and over in his mind. And before the start of the 1918 season, he made a decision.

"Babe, I'd like you to play some outfield for us this year," he said.

The big pitcher looked puzzled.

"You'd still be pitching, of course," Barrow continued. "But this club needs some more muscle at the plate and I think you're the guy to give it to us. How about it?"

65

"Why not," Babe said, flashing his big grin. He liked to hit and wouldn't mind getting a chance to belt a few more.

That year, the Babe appeared in ninety-five games, just twenty of them as a pitcher. He slammed out eleven home runs, good enough to tie him for the league lead. Barrow liked what he saw. The next season Babe pitched just seventeen times. He spent most of the season in the outfield and responded with twenty-nine homers, an all-time record up to 1919.

But the Sox didn't know the true value of their investment. On January 3, 1920, they sold the Babe to the New York Yankees and a whole new era in baseball was about to begin.

It started with a bang. Babe played rightfield for the Yanks (no pitching) and in 1920 belted an unheard of total of fifty-four home runs. His achievement was hailed as one of the most amazing of all time. In addition, the Bambino batted .376, proving he could do a lot more than just hit homers. The Babe was on his way.

Babe's arrival on the scene came just in time. During the 1919 World Series, several members of the Chicago White Sox had taken money from gamblers in return for not playing their best or trying real hard. They wanted to let Cincinnati win. The players involved in the infamous "Black Sox Scandal" were found out and banned from baseball for life. Many fans began wondering if the game were really honest after all.

At the different ballparks around the league, similar cries were heard coming from the stands.

Fix!

The game's crooked.

Who's paying you off for that one, ya bum!

It was on everyone's mind, and the fans began staying

away from the stadiums. Baseball could have been in real trouble—except for a man named Ruth who was hitting the ball out of sight with increasing regularity.

It has been said often that the Babe saved baseball. Maybe he didn't do it all by himself, but he surely had a large part in it. When he cracked out fifty-nine homers the next year, 1921, he was well on his way to becoming a living legend and the most popular player in the game.

These were the golden years. The Yankees were on the brink of becoming the best team in baseball, and the Babe was the toast of the town. He spent money as quickly as he made it. Between 1920 and 1929 he bought one or more Cadillacs a year. He hired private suites when the team was on the road, left ten dollar tips at the drop of a hat, broke training rules, and often refused to travel with the team.

It was a new-found freedom for a boy who had spent so many years confined to St. Mary's. Now the Babe wanted to live. And his thirst for the good things in life often got him into trouble with his teammates, managers, and even the commissioner of baseball.

But he was still hitting home runs. In addition to the 59 he belted in 1921, he had a .378 average and drove home 170 runs. He led the Yankees to the first pennant in the team's history. There was little doubt that Babe Ruth was a great, all-around ballplayer.

Success never stopped the Babe from getting in trouble. His manager, Miller Huggins, fined him on several occasions, and once had to suspend him. Judge Kennesaw Mountain Landis, the commissioner, had to suspend Babe and teammate Bob Meusel for a month at the beginning of the 1922 season because the two Yankees defied a ruling that prohibited World Series players from barnstorming (playing exhibition games for extra money) after the season ended.

When the Babe was suspended the fans went wild, calling for his reinstatement. They also called for Landis's scalp. When Ed Barrow, now with the Yanks, approached the commissioner, Landis said:

"I'm probably the most unpopular man in the country. But if you were in my shoes, what would you have done?"

Barrow snorted.

"I'd have suspended him, too."

But Babe rode out the storm, and by 1922 had his salary over the $50,000 mark. For those days it was a truly remarkable sum.

The Babe was worth every penny of it. Despite his off-field antics, he continued to crash monstrous home runs. In 1923, he batted .393, missing the coveted .400 circle by just seven percentage points. Then, in 1927, he set the greatest record of them all, playing with the greatest team of them all.

They called the Yankees of 1927 "Murderers Row." And what a formidable lot they were. Besides the Babe, there was a muscular young slugger named Lou Gehrig. Bob Meusel, Earle Combs, and Tony Lazzari were all solid .300 hitters. The team won 110 games and swept to the American League pennant.

For most of the season, Ruth and Gehrig were neck and neck in home runs. Then, in September, the Babe began to pull away. He hit two homers the second to last day of the season, giving him fifty-nine and tying his own record. The next day, facing lefty Tom Zachary of Washington, the Babe poked one high and deep into the rightfield stands. It was his sixtieth homer, a brand new record, and a fitting climax to a great season. Gehrig had forty-seven round trippers, and he and the Babe were now the most feared sluggers in baseball history.

The Yanks swept the World Series in four games that year. It was surely a high point for both the Babe and the Yanks. In a sense, it may have also signaled an end to the Babe's wild, carefree period.

Babe had married when he was a very young man. The marriage didn't work out, but being of the Catholic faith, he refused to consider divorce. In the meantime, he had fallen in love with Claire Hodgson, a southern girl who had been a part-time actress and model. When the first Mrs. Ruth died tragically in a fire, Babe and Claire were married. Claire proved to be a stabilizing influence on the big guy's life. The couple had two adopted daughters and Claire convinced Babe it was time to start saving money and thinking about the future.

The Babe was making about $75,000 when he married Claire in 1929, and was still at the top of the baseball world. But he was thirty-four years old and the end couldn't be far away. His thin legs were already showing signs of giving in, and Claire had to keep her husband from overeating and prod him to get into condition every spring.

There were still high spots. In the 1932 World Series, Babe came to bat against Charlie Root of the Chicago Cubs. The Babe had hit a homer earlier in the game and the Chicago fans were riding him mercilessly.

Let's see you hit another one, fatso.

You were lucky last time, Ruth. You're all washed up.

Come on, Charlie, fan the big bum.

Babe took two called strikes without moving a muscle and the Chicago fans howled even louder. Then he stepped out of the box and made a gesture toward the centerfield stands. Wrigley Field was in an uproar.

To this day there are those who call it coincidence, and those who say the Babe was actually pointing to the spot where he would hit the next pitch. At any rate, Root delivered and the Babe swung. There was the ball, rocketing on a line toward centerfield. It kept rising until it disappeared amidst the white-shirted fans in the bleachers.

As the Babe circled the bases, he grinned and taunted the Cub players in the field. The strange thing was that the fans who had been jeering him just moments ago were on their feet and cheering wildly.

That-a-boy, Babe.

You're the greatest, Babe, the greatest ever.

Babe Ruth had called his shot. The newspaper people went berserk. It was one of the most amazing things they had witnessed in all of sports.

But by now, it was getting harder and harder for the Babe to keep his body in shape. He was always prone to gaining weight, and his thin legs were having difficulty carrying his expanding midsection. He still could hit the ball a country mile, but it was tough doing it over the long season.

Thanks to Claire and his good friend and business manager, Christy Walsh, the Babe no longer had financial worries. Only he started thinking about something else.

Baseball was the only thing the Babe knew. He loved the game and wanted to stay in it. And he thought the best way to stay in it would be to manage his beloved Yankees. When he first brought up the possibility to the Yankee front office in 1932, he took them by surprise. They had never considered the Babe managerial timber. The reason was his antics as a rich young ballplayer.

"Ruth can't even manage himself. How do you expect him to manage a team of twenty-five other guys."

That became the standard line whenever Babe's name came out of a managerial pool. Though he had settled down, his past kept coming back to haunt him. His lack of discipline as a young man was all they remembered, not his growing maturity, dedication to baseball, and thorough knowledge of the game.

When the Yanks let Babe go at the end of the 1934 season, it looked like the end. He hated to admit it, and a vague promise of a managerial job led him to sign a contract with the Boston Braves for the 1935 season. Babe was now forty years old and obviously finished as a ballplayer. But the Braves wanted to exploit his name. That they did.

Then on a cool May afternoon in 1935, the Babe turned back the clock for the last time. Playing in Pittsburgh, the forty-year-old Sultan of Swat belted three long homers in three at-bats. The last was number 714 and the final four-bagger he would hit in the major leagues. Two weeks later he announced his retirement.

The Babe had money and fame, a wife who loved him, and many friends. He hunted and fished, and tried to enjoy a life of retirement. It was easy for him to make some money through endorsements or personal appearances. People were still willing to pay to see the portly ex-slugger hit a baseball.

But he wasn't happy. The Babe wanted a place in baseball as a manager. He spent the 1938 season as a coach with the Brooklyn Dodgers. Word had it that the Brooks would need a new manager the next year. The Babe's hopes rose. But then Leo Durocher, one of his few enemies, was appointed to the post, and the Babe was fired. That's the way Babe Ruth left baseball for the last time—fired.

His wife said that Babe would sometimes sit down and cry when the sport he'd helped save turned its back on him. Yet he kept waiting for a phone call that never came. He even swallowed his pride and begged the Yankee's for a chance to manage. Once more they said no. The Babe's final ambition was never to be realized.

Babe was still a young man when illness struck him down. Cancer of the throat was the diagnosis, and Babe spent his last years battling the dread disease. He returned to Yankee Stadium in 1948 for Babe Ruth Day, when his uniform with the number "3" was officially retired, and he was honored by many of his old teammates and friends.

Looking pale and wan, wearing his camel hair coat and cap, the Babe thanked everyone in a hoarse, tired voice. Despite what had happened to him in his retirement years, his final words to the huge, emotional crowd, showed no malice.

"To me," the Babe said, "the only real game in the world is baseball."

Then he said good-by, leaving a host of records and even more memories behind.

Babe Ruth died on August 17, 1948. He was fifty-three years old.

ROGERS HORNSBY
The Rajah
[1896–1963]

SOME MEN ARE born to be doctors, others politicians, still others jockeys, or steeplejacks, or actors. How many times have you heard someone say:

"Look at him. He was just born to do that!"

Rogers Hornsby was born to hit a baseball.

Fortunately for him, Rogers Hornsby lived in a land where baseball was looked upon as the national pastime. If he had lived in a land where they didn't play baseball, chances are he wouldn't have been happy.

That's a fairly safe assumption, because when Rogers Hornsby wasn't hitting a baseball, life just wasn't a fun thing for him. He never found anything comparable when his playing days were over. He argued with those around him, refused to listen to anyone, and never won over the people he managed. It was as if the Rajah blamed everyone else for the fact that age had caught up with him and he could no longer play.

When Rogers Hornsby came up to the plate, he'd set himself in the deepest corner of the batter's box and stride into the ball. With bat cocked, he'd level his eyes on the pitcher and wait. If the pitch was in the strike zone and he thought he could hit it, he'd step forward and lash out with a quick, extremely level swing.

The Rajah was a line drive hitter, spraying the ball to all fields, pounding as many doubles and triples to right center as to left center. It didn't matter that he was a right-handed hitter. He also had good power, but seldom hit long, high drives, like Babe Ruth or Mickey Mantle. His hits stayed low to the ground and traveled like bullets.

To this day, they call him the greatest right-handed hitter that ever lived. Perhaps that claim may be challenged, as men like Henry Aaron and Willie Mays wind up their careers. But in the Rajah's time, all the big hitters—Ruth, Gehrig, Cobb, Speaker, Joe Jackson, and later Ted Williams and Stan Musial—batted from the port side.

A look at the Rajah's batting record is evidence enough. The final totals can't be much more impressive. His lifetime batting average was .358, and that's topped by just one man: Ty Cobb. In the course of his career, Hornsby pounded out 2,930 base hits, had 541 doubles, 168 triples, and 302 home runs.

Of all Hornsby's accomplishments, one should be singled out. From 1921 to 1925, Rogers Hornsby went on the hottest batting tear of any player in history. His averages for those years were .397, .401, .384, .424, .403. It was utterly amazing.

During that period, the Rajah won five of his seven batting titles, reached the coveted .400 mark three times, including the highest mark in the twentieth century (.424), and he had a five-year batting average of .402. Considering there have been only a handful of .400 hitters in all of baseball, the last being Ted Williams in 1941, Hornsby's feat is even more memorable. For that five-year stretch, Rogers Hornsby hit a baseball better than any man who ever lived.

Born in the little town of Winters, Texas, on April 27, 1896, Rogers Hornsby geared his whole life to baseball. He played constantly as a youngster and demonstrated a keen batting eye almost from the first. In fact, it was his fine eyesight that he always credited with being a big plus factor in his hitting.

"Without these eyes of mine, I'm nothing," he once said. "They're my most valuable possession and I treat them with kid gloves."

Rajah wasn't kidding. From the time he was a youngster, he protected his eyes like a fanatic. While he was still in school, he often failed to complete reading assignments because he thought his eyes were being strained. If any of his friends were fooling around with a slingshot or some such threatening instrument, Rajah would make himself scarce in a hurry.

When he became a major league batting star, he was even more careful with his eyes. He never attended movies, very rarely read, even avoided smoke-filled rooms. Whether he benefited from the extracurricular eye care is hard to say. But no one will argue about his batting prowess and "good eye" for the strike zone.

By 1914, the Rajah was a skinny eighteen-year-old shortstop, good enough to play for Hugo-Denison of the Texas-Oklahoma League. Not yet fully grown or matured, he batted just .232 in 113 games, showing little of the stick that was to take him into the Hall of Fame.

The next year he did a little better, climbing to a .277 mark, when the St. Louis Cardinals bought his contract for $500. Miller Huggins was managing the Cards then, and he needed a shortstop, the position Hornsby was playing in the minors.

"Kid, you look like you'll bend in a stiff wind, and we get

a lot of them around here," little Hug scowled. "Try to beef up some during the off-season."

After hitting just .246 in the final eighteen games for the Cards, Rajah went back to his uncle's farm in Texas, determined to take the little manager's advice. He worked hard and ate hearty, going from 130 to 160 pounds. When he returned to spring training in 1916, he sought out his manager.

"Try this shortstop on for size," he said proudly.

"You'll do," said Hug, grinning a little. "Now we'll see if you can hit."

No one would ever ask that question again. The Rajah began leveling National League pitching from the start, hitting a robust .313, and driving in sixty runs. But he was still learning his trade, and being shifted around to the three different infield positions didn't help, either. The next three seasons he batted .327, .281, and .318, and no one was more disappointed than he was.

"I know I can hit better than this," he told a teammate. "And I'm gonna show these guys what I mean very soon."

The year was 1920, and Hornsby was about to warm up for the greatest five-year batting streak ever. He hit a cool .370 that season, collecting 218 hits and driving home 94 runs. It was a foreshadowing of things to come.

Rajah was also settled in the field, having found a home at second base. There were slicker fielders around, but Hornsby made all the plays. Staying in one infield position stabilized his game and enabled him to concentrate more at the plate.

When Rog batted .397 the next year, everyone stood up and took notice. In addition to his skyrocketing batting average, his homer total zoomed from nine to twenty-one, and his RBI's led the league at 126. In 1922, he was even better, winning the National League triple crown with a .401 batting average, 42 homers, and 152 runs batted in. Hornsby was in the groove. He had 250 base hits that year, just seven short of the major league record. It might have been his finest season ever. But unlike some of the other greats of the era, there were no garlands of roses placed upon the Rajah's head. His popularity was always far below his batting average.

One reason was the Hornsby personality. He was straightforward and to the point. As for tact, he had none. He wanted things his way and was moved to insult and sarcasm when someone went against his judgment.

There were just two kinds of persons Hornsby treated with respect—kids and umpires. The Rajah always had a soft spot for the little ones, and took time to talk and joke with them whenever he had the chance. With the umps, it was a matter of mutual respect. Early in his career, Rog was angered by a call and slugged one of the men in blue. Soon after, he realized that this kind of action was fruitless.

"The umpires don't lose games for you," he'd often growl. "You lose them yourself."

As for the umps, they knew Rog was as honest and straight as he was outspoken. A pitcher once questioned a close pitch that he thought should have been a third strike on Rajah. The great Bill Klem, calling them behind the plate, said no. When, on the next pitch, Hornsby tagged one, Klem is reputed to have told the pitcher,

"Here's some advice, son. When you throw a strike to Hornsby, he's the first to let you know about it."

Near the end of the 1925 season, Hornsby's career was at its peak. It was his fifth straight big season and many people were beginning to call him the greatest hitter who ever lived. That, perhaps, was one of the reasons Cardinal-owner Sam Breadon appointed him playing manager of the team.

"I'm no manager," Hornsby roared in protest. "I don't want the job. Get someone else!"

Inwardly, the Rajah knew he wasn't cut out for the job. But Breadon insisted and the Hornsby pride showed through. While he knew he didn't want the job, he couldn't think of anyone who could do it better. In his first meeting as manager of the Redbirds, he kicked aside a blackboard that had been used in the clubhouse.

"No more of this stuff around here. If I need a blackboard to show a guy how to play this game, I don't want him on my team."

My team. That's how Rog envisioned the Cards when he took over. That's how he saw all the teams he was to manage. General managers and owners were fine, but only if they kept their noses out of his business.

But Breadon's choice was vindicated the next year, 1926, when Hornsby piloted the Cards to their first National League pennant. Running the team from his second-base position and trying to handle all the managerial responsibility, the Rajah lost some of his concentration at the plate. His average dipped to .317, but he still managed to knock in ninety-three runs. More importantly, the team won.

The World Series that followed was one of the classics. The Cards faced the powerful New York Yankees, just a year away from their Murderers' Row season of 1927. The Bronx Bombers featured the likes of Ruth, Gehrig, Meusel, Combs, Lazzari. They seemed unbeatable.

For six games, the two teams battled to a stalemate. The Rajah didn't do much with his bat, hitting just .250 for the Series, but he made a decision in the seventh game that took courage and perhaps an innate sixth sense for the game.

The Cards were leading, 3-2, going into the seventh inning.

But Redbird starter Jess Haines was suddenly losing his stuff. With two out, the Yanks loaded the bases. Haines called Hornsby to the mound.

"Rog, this hand is killing me," he said. "I can't go on."

He showed the manager a huge blister that had developed on his index finger. Hornsby took one look at it and shouted in the direction of his bullpen.

"Get Alex ready."

Alex was the immortal Grover Cleveland Alexander, one of the greatest pitchers in National League history. But Alexander was thirty-nine years old and considered over the hill. He also had a fondness for the bottle that had increased with age. Picked up by the Cards in mid-season, Alexander won some key games and finished with a 12-10 record.

Then, in the Series, the old man had turned back the clock and won two games, including the sixth game the day before. Figuring he wouldn't be pitching in the finale, Alex went out and hoisted a few, quite a few, the night before.

When Hornsby saw one of his bullpen catchers motioning to him, he trotted down.

"I don't think Alex can pitch, Rog," said the man.

"Why not?" growled Hornsby, his keen eyes squinting in anger.

"Well, he must have tied on a pretty good one last night. He's been dozing most of the game."

Hornsby walked over to Alex, still half-sleeping on a chair.

"Get up and start throwing. You're coming in for Haines."

"I don't know, Rog," answered Alex, sheepishly.

"I do," snapped Hornsby, settling the matter right there.

Minutes later, Alexander was on the mound facing Tony Lazzari, the Yankees brilliant young second baseman. A hit here and the Yanks would win it.

Playing before a sellout crowd at Yankee Stadium, Alex went to work, Hornsby shouting encouragement from second.

The old pro's first pitch was a strike; then Lazzari smacked a hard liner down the leftfield line. For a second, it looked as if it would clear the bases. Then it hooked foul. Alexander and the Cards had a reprieve.

The next pitch just missed for a ball. Alex took a deep breath, then kicked and fired. Lazzari went after the breaking ball and missed it. He was out. Alex had done it. For the next two innings, the old hurler held the Yanks hitless, and the Cardinals were world champions. Alex was the hero, Hornsby the guiding genius, and everyone in St. Louis was happy.

It was to be the highlight of Rajah's managerial career. Although no one knew it at the time, Hornsby and Breadon had clashed severely over an exhibition game somehow scheduled right in the midst of the 1926 pennant run. The Card owner was hurt by his manager's sharp tongue. Champions or no, he realized that the combination couldn't continue.

He broke it by offering Rog a one-year contract for the 1927 season, instead of the customary three-year pact. When Hornsby balked, he found himself traded to the Giants for another second baseman, Frankie Frisch, and a second-rank pitcher. Breadon's neck was saved by Frisch, the Fordham Flash, who turned out to be almost as brilliant a performer as Hornsby.

Relieved of managerial responsibility, Rog bounced back at the plate, hitting .361 with 26 homers and 125 RBI's. It looked as if he had found a home. But no, once again his stubborn manner and outspoken ways got him into trouble. Taking over the club for a few days when Manager McGraw was absent, Rajah insisted on doing things his way, even though some were directly opposite to McGraw's. He also avoided Giants' owner Horace Stoneham as you'd avoid the plague. The tactless Rog made it so obvious that Stoneham wondered what he had done to make the superstar dislike him.

The result was another trade, this time to the Boston Braves. There Rog found a man he actually liked, the Braves' owner, Judge Emil Fuchs. Happy in Boston, he hit a ton, and was named playing manager at the end of May. His .387 average was shades of the old Hornsby, all right, but the Braves had a poor team, and after the season Fuchs couldn't turn down an offer of five players and $200,000 from the Cubs. They wanted Hornsby.

In Chicago, his fourth team in four years, Rog took up right where he had left off, having one of his greatest seasons at the plate. His 1929 stats were a .380 batting average, 40 home runs, and 149 RBI's. Not surprisingly, the Cubs won the National League pennant.

But in the series, the Cubs were demolished by the Philadelphia A's, four games to one. Rog batted just .238, knocked in one run, and struck out eight times. He didn't know it then, but that Series was the start of more troubles to come.

When Cub Manager Joe McCarthy resigned to go over to the Yankees, Hornsby got the job. But the tough times were coming. Rajah lost a bundle of money in the stock market crash of 1929, then broke a leg at the outset of the 1930 season. When recovered, he developed a painful heel spur that later required surgery. He'd never be 100 per cent sound on the diamond again.

The Rajah hit .331 in 1931, with ninety RBI's in just one

hundred games. He was thirty-five now, and he'd never play that many games again. The next year he appeared in just nineteen contests, batted .224, and lost his managing job when the season ended.

Hornsby had a long-standing love of gambling, and his habit of betting on the horses led him into trouble first with Cubs General Manager Bill Veeck, and then with Baseball Commissioner Landis. The first encounter resulted in Rogers' losing his job, the second in a verbal exchange with the Commissioner that made all the front pages.

Hornsby's life was cascading down around him. He was broke, being sued for divorce, out of a job, slowed to a walk by the heel spur, and seemingly unable to get along with anyone. His old friend at the Cardinals, Branch Rickey, called Rog back as a pinch-hitter and part-timer. It must have been painful for the proud Hornsby to accept, but he did, and batted .325 in a minor role, coming to bat just forty-six times. It was plain that he was finished.

But the Rajah knew nothing but baseball, so he hung on. He was named manager of the American League's St. Louis Browns in 1933, working for another owner he liked, Phil Ball. He pinch-hit very infrequently and usually worked the third-base coaching box. He still liked being on the field, though he always walked with a noticeable limp.

When Ball died, the Browns got a new owner, Donald Barnes, plus a general manager, Bill DeWitt. Hornsby still hated general managers. He thought they interfered with his running of the ball club. The trouble started. Finally, Barnes called Rog on the carpet about his gambling. In his not-so-polite fashion, Rog told Barnes to mind his own business. The words became harsher and Hornsby was fired. It was 1937 and he was forty-one years old. He had come to the plate fifty-six times that year and batted .321.

From there, he managed in the minors, on and off, until 1952. His final big league jobs were with the Browns and Cincinnati Reds. Each lasted less than a year.

By then, Hornsby was colder and more impersonal than ever. He was the only manager who didn't walk out to the mound to console a pitcher he was removing. A curt gesture from the dugout was all the effort he expended, as if to say, "You couldn't do the job, so get out of there on your own." Ballplayers were more sensitive than they had been in his day. They didn't understand the old man, who once said:

"You don't have to tell me. The manager comes last as far as the players are concerned." Maybe he should have looked twice.

His last years were difficult and lonely. He still gambled on the horses and insulted too many people around him. He married three times, divorced twice, and had two sons. Yet it didn't satisfy him. When he died of a heart attack at the age of sixty-seven in 1963, those who knew him said he was an unhappy man.

Rogers Hornsby brought much of his trouble on himself. In his prime, during that incredible five-year stretch, he was the most devastating hitter who ever lived. Had his career not been cut short by leg injuries, his records would have undoubtedly been even greater. As a part-time and injured player, he had to lose points from his lifetime average. Healthy, he would have challenged Cobb's .367, and maybe surpassed it.

There was once a flicker of compassion in the man who was his own worst enemy. Asked by a reporter if there had been pitchers he feared, Hornsby flashed his dimpled grin and said:

"Nope, I felt sorry for all of them."

With Rogers Hornsby batting, everyone else did, too.

Ty Cobb

Detroit Tigers

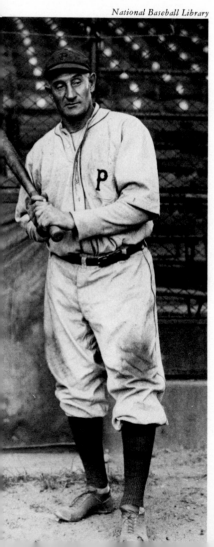

National Baseball Library

Honus Wagner

Cleveland Indians

Tris Speaker

Tris Speaker

National Baseball Library

Christy Mathewson

WALTER JOHNSON

National Baseball Library

New York Yankees

BABE RUTH

LOU GEHRIG

New York Yankees

ROGERS HORNSBY

HENRY LOUIS GEHRIG
The Iron Horse

[1903–1941]

Lou GEHRIG NEVER asked much from life. The perfect day for Lou was to leave home in the morning, play a baseball game in the afternoon, and return for a big meal in the evening. That's what made him happy.

But it wasn't always that simple. Lou Gehrig paid a price to achieve his goals. He worked long and hard to become tops at his game. When he made it, he had to contend with the fame that accompanies a public celebrity and national hero. And finally, he had to cope with having all this taken from him in the cruelest of ways while he was still in his prime.

Yet Lou Gehrig never complained. The famed Iron Horse of the New York Yankees took the bitter with the sweet, and is remembered today as one of the most beloved figures ever to participate in the national pastime.

Lou played fourteen full seasons with the Yankees. In that time, he never missed a ball game. Not one! Lou's unbelievable record of 2,130 consecutive games is a mark that will likely never be broken. And during those years, the left-handed hitting first baseman compiled a lifetime batting average of .340, clubbed out 494 home runs, and drove 1,991 runs across the plate. He set many more records, some of which still stand today.

The Lou Gehrig story is truly an American story, a rags to riches saga, where hard work and sweat were the means, and starring in the game of baseball the end. But as with most success stories, there were humble beginnings.

Henry Louis Gehrig was born on June 19, 1903, in New York City. His parents, Christina and Heinrich Gehrig, were German immigrants, and their native tongue was the first that Lou spoke. Perhaps that's one of the common bonds that always kept him so close to his parents. He was to cherish and care for them the rest of his life.

Little Louie, as his mother called him, knew the taste of poverty. His father took jobs wherever they were offered and was occasionally out of work for short periods of time. Lou's mother took very good care of the boy. Her two other children both died in infancy, and she wanted to be sure her Louie was strong and healthy—which he was.

When he was five, Lou got a Christmas present he never forgot—a catcher's mitt. He was left-handed, and the mitt was made for a righty, but it didn't matter. As soon as the warm weather came, young Lou was out on the sandlots, playing baseball with the other boys. He was always big and strong, chunky of build, and could compete with boys two and three years older.

One day Lou came in hot and dusty from the afternoon's play, and his mother asked, "Louie, do you really like this game you always play?"

"Yes, Mama," young Lou answered. "I like it better than anything else."

But Lou liked school, too. His grades were always good and he hated to miss a day. In fact, he once sneaked off to school after the doctor told his mother he had a touch of pneumonia. The only way the principal could get him to go home was to promise to mark him present even though he was out. Lou was an every-day man already.

By the time Lou was ten or eleven, he was already a good ballplayer. But he also spent time working in a delicatessen and doing odd jobs around the neighborhood. He was known as a good kid and everyone liked him.

His mother got a job as cook and housekeeper at one of the fraternity houses at Columbia University. The job would ultimately help Lou enter Columbia as a freshman in 1920. By then, Lou had already acquired some baseball glory. His Police Athletic League team traveled to Chicago to play a team from that city, and Lou responded with a grand slam home run. He was thinking baseball as a career.

But he entered Columbia at his mother's insistence. His father had fallen ill and Lou wanted to quit school to help support the family. Fortunately, he didn't.

Nothing came easily for Lou. At Columbia, he had to work very hard at his studies. And when he went out for the football and baseball teams, he had to work very hard to master the fundamentals of both games. He wasn't a naturally quick thinker and didn't react instinctively on the ballfield. He had to study and practice, practice and learn, practice and perfect before he did things consistently. But the one thing that made him outstanding was his hitting.

He practiced that, too. It wasn't long before his powerful shoulders and arms, and his thick legs, were working together, enabling him to clout the ball harder than anyone else. And the word was getting out.

"This Gehrig kid at Columbia can hit a ton," said one old scout.

"Yeah, but he's not interested in the big leagues," said another. "I hear his mother doesn't want him to play."

The scouts were right. His parents didn't understand baseball and couldn't see how a man made a living at it. But once again fate intervened. Lou's father needed an operation very badly. Then his mother fell ill with double pneumonia. Lou needed money. The one way to get it was to sign a baseball contract. It was the Yankees who made the best offer so Lou signed for a $1,500 bonus and a salary of $3,000 a year.

Lou was painfully shy when he joined the Yankees in 1923. Here he was, sitting alongside Babe Ruth and all the other players he'd idolized over the years. He didn't know what to say or do. When someone spoke to him, his answers were usually brief—yes, sir, or no, sir.

The first time he got into a game, he took three cuts and was struck out. Still shaking from excitement, he returned to the bench. The only seat available was next to the great Babe. Lou sat down, head bowed. Suddenly he felt a friendly hand on his shoulder.

"Don't worry about it, kid," said the Babe in his gruff, cracking voice. "You took some good cuts. You just didn't connect. Next time around you'll get hold of one."

Babe was right. The next time Lou got into a game, he slammed a solid double down the rightfield line for his first big league hit. But he had a lot to learn. He didn't know about running the bases, and he was still very clumsy around first base and in the field. The other players called him "Tanglefoot."

The Yankees wanted the big kid's bat, all right, but nevertheless Lou spent the better part of the 1923 and 1924 seasons at Hartford in the Eastern League.

At Hartford, Lou worked and worked. For hours on end he'd scoop up ground balls at first base, and practice taking throws in the dirt. He also had to learn how to use his feet around the bag, and what to do when there were men on base. None of these things came easily to him.

Gradually, Lou began to improve. And the more confidence he had in the field, the more noise he made at the plate, ripping line drives all over the field, and belting long homers into the distant stands. His manager at Hartford, Pat O'Connor, knew that he had a good one on his hands. He gave Lou some advice.

"Baseball is a five month season," he told Lou. "Put everything you have into those five months and you'll be better off. You'll meet plenty of party boys in the majors. Be smart; tell 'em to take a walk."

It was good advice. In fact, the Babe himself once suggested that Lou keep in top condition.

"I didn't," said the Babe, "and the older I get, the more I pay for it."

Lou listened and learned. He always kept himself in top shape. During the season he concentrated on baseball, keeping both mentally and physically ready to play. He rarely drank or smoked, ate well, and got plenty of sleep. He was the model of what a ballplayer should be.

In 1925, Lou was back with the Yankees for good. For awhile, he sat the bench, just pinch-hitting and playing occasionally. Then on June 2, Manager Miller Huggins wrote Lou's name into the starting lineup. First baseman Wally Pipp had a headache and couldn't play.

"You're in there today, Lou," said Huggins, matter-offactly. "Do the job right and you'll stay there."

Lou swallowed hard. This was his big chance. He wondered if he'd pass the test or succumb to his former clumsy ways.

He needn't have worried. Young Lou started the game and also began his famous streak. He wouldn't miss another game for more than fourteen years.

Lou played in 126 games that first year. He batted a respectable .295, clubbed twenty-one homers, and drove in sixty-eight runs. It would be the only time in his great career that he'd bat in fewer than one hundred runs.

It wasn't long before the Yankees had set their lineup. Ruth batted third and Lou right behind him. There has never been a pair of sluggers batting together who could match them. But if either of them had an advantage, it had to be the Babe.

At one time, the hurlers had worked around the mighty Ruth—given him bad pitches. A walk was better than a home run. Now, with the dangerous Gehrig behind him, the Babe got more pitches to hit. And when the Babe did connect for one of his huge home runs, the pitcher would likely take his wrath out on the next batter, Gehrig.

But nothing fazed Lou. He batted over .300 the next season and drove in more than one hundred runs. He helped the Yankees win the pennant. Still, it didn't give much of a hint as to what was coming the next year.

Lou, Babe, and the rest of the Yankees started the 1927 season as if they wanted to tear the baseball world apart. That they did. The team won 110 games and took the American League pennant in a breeze. Lou and the Babe led the parade of potent bats known as "Murderers Row." Many fans still call the 1927 Yanks the greatest team ever to step onto a diamond.

Both Lou and the Babe created great copy all season long. They were both hitting home runs as if this was the last season ever. They went over the twenty mark together, then passed thirty, neck and neck.

"What are you trying to do, kid," the Babe joked at midseason, "break my record?"

Lou grinned. "Naw, Babe. I just figure if I hit a few now and then, you'll get mad and hit a few more."

The sluggers were good friends and rooted for each other. There was never any jealousy between them. When they approached and reached the forty mark at about the same time, it was a question as to who would hit more. September provided the difference. The Babe went on another tear, while Lou slowed his pace. When it was over, the Babe was a national hero with a new record of sixty homers, and many people were quick to forget that Lou Gehrig wasn't far behind with forty-seven.

In addition, Lou batted a sensational .373 and drove in a record 175 runs. But almost all was lost in the Babe's glory, and the Yankees' subsequent sweep of the World Series.

It got to be old hat to Lou. He was destined to play much of his career in the largest shadow ever cast in baseball—the shadow of Babe Ruth. Everything about the Babe attracted the fans. People were drawn to him and he loved people. He played to the crowds like a famous actor working to an audience. He had them in the palms of his hands.

Lou, by contrast, lacked all of the Babe's flair. He had a strong, thick body, and movie-star looks. But his innate shyness and lack of a public image kept him out of the limelight.

People liked him, but not with the Ruthian passion. And Lou never went out of his way to attract attention. His business was baseball. And it took all his concentration to play it well.

Even his home runs lacked the verve of the Babe's. When Ruth hit one, the ball sailed higher and higher, deeper and deeper. Fans followed it as they'd follow the flight of a bird. The Babe hit majestic clouts, home runs that would never be forgotten.

Lou probably hit the baseball harder. But he almost always hit bullets, line drives that reached their destination in a matter of seconds. There was no majestic flow. The ball simply rocketed on a straight line into the seats. If you looked away for a second, you might miss it. There wasn't time to get excited, stand up, scream and yell. Lou just hit the ball and it stayed hit.

Off the field, Lou continued to live a quiet, almost sheltered life. He bought a home in New Rochelle, New York, for his parents and moved in with them. He still loved his mother's cooking and liked to be around to look after the two aging Gehrigs.

Lou finally married in 1933, after his bride, Eleanor Twitchell of Chicago, had waited four years for him to pop the question. His shyness prevented the words from coming on many occasions. But even after marriage, he preferred the home life, staying close to his mother, and even bringing Eleanor's mother East to be near them.

The years were rolling on now. The Babe was fading and finally left the Yankees in 1934. Now Lou was Number One. The cheers were louder and longer with each passing game.

Come on, Lou, clout one!

Bust that fence down, Lou baby.

Hit it down his throat, Loooooie.

There hadn't been too much of that when the Babe was around, and even now much of Lou's great play and consistency was taken for granted. He was never a spectacular fielder, but through constant trial and error, and hours of practice, had become dependable and proficient. Now he didn't have to worry about the rest of his game. He could concentrate on his hitting.

And hit he did. There were batting averages of .374, .379, .363, and .354. He clubbed forty-nine homers on two occasions, had forty-seven and forty-six in two other years. He set a new record with 184 RBI's, and in other seasons drove in 175, 174, 165, 159, 152, 151. He was probably the most consistent RBI man of all time.

But Lou could never grab the spotlight for long. He did it once in 1932 when he banged out four home runs in four consecutive times at bat. He was the first ballplayer in the twentieth century to accomplish that feat. But that same year when he cracked two home runs in one Series game against the Cubs, he happened to pick the same game where the Babe called his famous shot. Lou's homers were forgotten.

Lou's shyness prevented him from making too many endorsements. One time he was going to plug a breakfast cereal, Huskies, on the radio. Lou couldn't handle the script, and it was decided that he'd say just one word, the name of the product. Lou was nervous when he went to the studio. The announcer gave it the buildup, then said:

"And what is it that gives you, Lou Gehrig, the get-up and go to play great baseball every day?"

Lou was set. He gave his answer.

"Wheaties!"

The whole studio broke up. Lou had named Huskies' biggest rival for the breakfast market. But because it was Lou, no one really got mad.

Lou's top baseball salary was about $35,000, roughly half of what the Babe made, but he didn't care. He thought that was plenty, and he saved his money faithfully, never having financial worries in his life. He and the Babe often went barnstorming together and picked up good bundles of change that way. Lou even ventured to Hollywood and made a movie, a western in which he played—of all people—himself.

So while his popularity lacked the wild flamboyance of Ruth's, it nevertheless existed. And as his career drew on, there was more and more talk about the streak.

Lou hadn't missed a game since he first broke into the lineup for good in 1925. He played with an assortment of ailments and injuries. It became a personal challenge to him, just like attending school had been so many years before.

He broke the old record, held by former Yankee Everett Scott, midway through his career, and soon it became a matter of how far he could go. On more than one occasion he defied doctor's orders and went out to the ballpark, then talked his manager into putting his name in the lineup. In his quiet way, Lou Gehrig had as much courage as any man who ever lived.

It wasn't too much longer before his courage was put to the ultimate test. Lou had another fine year in 1937. He hit .351, spanked out thirty-seven homers, and drove home 159 runs. He was thirty-four years old, but seemed to be still in his prime. Baseball men were predicting a slew of records before he was through.

Then in 1938 he started terribly. By the time he picked up the pace, it was mid-season. He finished with a .295 average, twenty-nine homers, and 114 RBI's. The totals represented the lowest in more than a decade. Whispers started going around the league that the big guy was losing it. He didn't seem to have the same bounce anymore. Sure, he still hit. His statistics would please many a major leaguer today. But it wasn't the real Gehrig.

Lou was also concerned. He was determined to get himself into top shape for the 1939 season. He was convinced that everything would come back. He and Eleanor left for Florida early.

But the spring was a struggle for Lou. He seemed to lose more of his timing. He couldn't make routine plays in the field. The great Ty Cobb, watching the Yankees work out, noticed Lou and said:

"I've seen a lot of these big guys go. When they fall apart, it happens overnight."

Still, Lou refused to believe it. His manager, Joe McCarthy, also defended him.

"Lou stays in the lineup until he takes himself out," McCarthy told an inquisitive press corps.

Lou played the first eight games of the 1939 season. He made just four hits in twenty-eight at-bats, all singles, for an average of .143. In the eighth game he made a very routine play in the field, though it seemed to take a great effort for him to do it. As he returned to the dugout, a teammate put his arm around the big slugger.

"Nice play, Lou," he said.

That did it. On May 2, Lou approached his manager in a hotel lobby. He spoke slowly.

"Joe, I'm not helping the team anymore. It's not fair to the other guys for me to keep going. I want you to take me out."

When Lou, as Yankee captain, walked up to home plate that afternoon with the Yankee lineup card, there were tears in his eyes. His name was missing for the first time in fourteen years. He returned to the dugout and watched others play the game he loved so much.

A short time later he went to the famed Mayo Clinic in Minnesota for a complete physical examination. The result came as a shock to the entire baseball world.

Lou Gehrig, the Iron Horse, was suffering from a rare disease called amyotrophic lateral sclerosis. It caused a hardening of the spinal cord and gradual deterioration of the entire muscle system. It was irreversible, and in all cases fatal. Lou learned all this on his thirty-sixth birthday.

It wasn't kept a secret. The whole country knew of Lou's illness. But he didn't just quit, though he could no longer play baseball. He was offered a job with the New York City Parole Board. He took it, studied hard the things he'd have to know, and worked at it every day for as long as his health permitted.

At first Lou was optimistic. He somehow hoped he'd play baseball again, but he knew he might not.

"Maybe I won't play again," he would often say, "but I've had fourteen seasons in the big leagues and I'm thankful for every one of them. I've got no kick."

The tributes began pouring in. The Baseball Hall of Fame at Cooperstown, New York, waived a standing rule to make room for Lou in 1939, the same year he retired. The Yankees told him no one would ever wear his number 4 uniform again, and no other ballplayer would ever use his locker in the Yankee clubhouse.

On July 4, 1939, the Yankees gave Lou a day. The big stadium was packed to the rafters as many of Lou's teammates returned to honor him. The Babe was there, and he came out and threw his arms around his old slugging mate in one of the most moving moments in all sports.

Then Lou stepped nervously to the microphone. In his halting, humble way, he spoke of all the things he loved in life—his wife, his parents, baseball, the Yankees. Choked with emotion he thanked everyone for the things they'd done for him. When he was almost finished, he looked around the saddened stadium and spoke to his fans for the last time. His words will always be remembered.

"I may have been given a bad break, but today I consider myself the luckiest man on the face of the earth."

As the cheers descended upon him, Lou Gehrig walked slowly to the Yankee dugout and disappeared into the runway. It was over for the Iron Horse.

Lou fought a gallant battle against the disease that robbed him of his career and everything else he had to live for. No one with his illness had ever lived more than two years. Lou broke that record by a month.

He died quietly on June 2, 1941, just sixteen years to the day he'd started his record-breaking streak of consecutive baseball games.

JOSEPH PAUL DIMAGGIO

The Yankee Clipper

[1914–   ]

MORE THAN 67,000 rabid baseball fans jammed into Cleveland's Municipal Stadium on the night of July 17, 1941. It was an unbelievable crowd for a mid-season ball game, and a casual observer might have wondered why the people had turned out in such force.

But Cleveland's own Indians were playing the Yankees that night, and wherever the Bronx Bombers had been for the past several weeks, a huge crowd was sure to follow.

There was good reason for it. Joe DiMaggio, the Yanks' slugging young centerfielder, was in the midst of setting one of the greatest baseball records of all time.

Coming into the Cleveland game, DiMaggio had hit safely in fifty-six consecutive baseball games! He had already broken the old record of forty-four, set back in 1897 by Wee Willie Keeler. Now it was a matter of how far the famed Yankee Clipper could go.

The streak had started back on May 15. For more than two months after that, DiMag collected at least one hit in every game he played. The pressure was unbearable, even after the record fell.

How long can he go?

That question was on everyone's mind. The Clipper's streak had received immense press coverage and the whole nation was caught up in the growing drama.

"He hasn't even broken his own record yet," one story related. "This kid once hit in 61 straight in the minor leagues."

This was true, too. It seems that DiMaggio's quick bat was always hard to silence.

Batting against lefty Al Smith in the first that July 17, 1941, the Yankee Clipper hit a shot down the third-base line. It looked like another hit. But Cleveland third baseman Ken Keltner made a backhanded stop and threw DiMag out at first.

When Joe came up in the fourth, Smith worked carefully and walked the Clipper. Then in the seventh, Joe hit another shot toward third. Again, Keltner came up with a fine play and threw his man out at first. Now the tension was building. Joe might not get another chance to hit.

But the Yanks rallied in the eighth, scoring two runs. Sure enough, Joe would get another crack at keeping the streak alive. When he came up, there was a right-handed relief pitcher on the mound. His name was Jim Bagby, and he was perfectly aware of the situation. On a half-dozen previous occasions during the two-month-old streak, DiMag had waited until his last at-bat to hit safely.

The Cleveland fans were aware, too. They fell into a strange silence as Joe took his position in the batter's box. He stood deep, as usual, bat held high, moving ever so slightly.

He got his pitch from Bagby and went after it. *Crack!* It had the good sound. But the ball rocketed straight at shortstop Lou Boudreau, who picked it up and started a double-play.

As DiMag trotted slowly back to the dugout, the big

crowd erupted with a standing ovation. It was a fitting tribute to the man who had just set one of the greatest of all
baseball records.

"I had no regrets when the streak ended," Joe D. said later.
"It was a great two months for me and the Yanks had just
about wrapped up the pennant when it ended."

In fact, so casually did Joe take the finish of the streak that
the next day he went out and started another skein that lasted
for sixteen games.

Joe's statistics during the long streak were eye-opening. He
came to bat 223 times from May to July, and had 91 hits for
a .408 average. He whacked out 15 homers, drove in 55 runs,
and scored 56 times. He also had four triples, 16 doubles, and
walked 21 times. The Yankee Clipper was the talk of the
American League . . . and all of baseball.

But then, Joe DiMaggio had always been a great ballplayer, right from the time he entered the minor leagues.
When he joined the Yankees in 1936, he had some very big
shoes to fill. Though Babe Ruth was already gone, his Yankee
legend would always remain. The amazing Lou Gehrig was
still driving home runs, but it would be only a few short
years before illness would force him out of the game.

Then it would be up to DiMag to lead the Yankee dynasty
through the 1940's. He'd be the superstar upon whom the
team would build, the one they'd rally around. And he'd do
his job well.

Joseph Paul DiMaggio was born in Martinez, California, on
November 25, 1914. His father, Giuseppe, worked as a fisherman, and his mother, Rosalie, spent her time caring for the
nine DiMaggio children. The last three born—Vince, Joe,
and Dom—were the three who eventually played major

league baseball.

When asked about his childhood, Joe always says his first memory was the smell of fish. But young Joe never really liked the aroma that put food in all their mouths. In fact, one reason he first started playing baseball was to get out of helping his father with the fishing and with cleaning the boat.

Though his father worked hard, the family had little more than the basic essentials for living. Their house was small, and the five boys slept in one room, the four girls in another. Since there were three boys before Joe, he wore hand-me-downs most of his young life. But it didn't matter, the boys had fun working and playing together.

The funny thing was that once Giuseppe DiMaggio stopped asking his young son to help with the boat, Joe stopped playing ball and got a job selling papers. But soon, older brother Vince began to show some real promise as a ballplayer. He had quit high school to work, but still played on Sundays. Pretty soon he signed with the San Francisco Seals of the Pacific Coast League, and was sent to play at Tucson.

Young Joe watched Vince's progress and came to an obvious conclusion.

"If Vince could make money playing ball, I figured I could, too," Joe said. "I was pretty cocky, then, and I didn't think it would be difficult."

Pretty soon, Joe began to follow in Vince's footsteps. And the first thing he did was quit high school after two years.

"I didn't really enjoy school then," he says. "Vince quit because the family needed money. I quit because I wanted to. If I had it to do all over again, I'd certainly stick with it a lot longer."

But soon after he left school, his baseball career started to move right along. First it was a Boys' Club team, then a semi-pro team called Sunset Produce. And Joe produced, all right, a .632 batting average in eighteen games. He played short and third with the Sunsets, and soon after received his first pro offer from the San Francisco Missions of the Pacific Coast League.

The Missions offered Joe $150 per month, more money than he'd ever made in his life. But before he could put on a Missions uniform, something else happened. Joe went out to watch brother Vince play with the Seals, who were also in the Pacific Coast League, and a Seals scout, Spike Hennessey, recognized him and introduced him to Manager Ike Caveney. Joe had a tryout and was added to the team. Since the Seals had a better reputation than the Missions, he signed with them for $250 per month.

He made his debut at the tail end of the 1932 season. He wasn't even eighteen yet, but the Seals needed a shortstop to fill in for the final three games of the year. When he came up for the first time there were some murmurs in the crowd.

Hey, ain't that Vince's brother?

Another DiMag. Let's go, you DiMag!

Joe was nervous. He could feel himself shaking inside. He looked out at the mound toward veteran pitcher Ted Pillette. He got ready. When Pillette came in with a fastball, Joe swung and sent a shot rocketing off the leftfield fence. By the time the ball was retrieved, Joe's long stride had taken him all the way around to third. He had himself a triple in his first at-bat with the Seals.

The next season, Joe was back, but Augie Galan, the regular shortstop, had reclaimed the infield job. Joe sat the bench for a few games. Then Manager Caveney decided to try the youngster in right field. He was to remain there the rest of the year.

Soon after getting into the lineup, Joe began to hit. And hit . . . and hit . . . and hit. Before long, he was building a long streak. When it reached fifty games, the mayor of San Francisco gave him a gold watch. And when it was finally stopped at sixty-one, the whole league was singing the praises of the tall, thin 18-year-old outfielder.

DiMag batted .340 that year, playing an expanded schedule of 187 games. That's a lot of baseball. And he banged out 259 hits, 28 homers, and drove in a league-leading 169 runs.

It looked like more of the same the next year, but torn knee tendons slowed his pace, and he hit .341 in just 101 games.

Because of the knee injury, several teams that had been interested in DiMag backed off. Now only the Yankees remained. When the negotiating ended, it was agreed that the Yanks would pay $25,000 plus five players for Joe's services. In addition, he was to remain with the Seals for the 1935 season and receive regular treatments on the knee.

As the Yanks watched developments in San Francisco during that season, they began to lick their chops. With no obvious effects from the knee injury, DiMag was going berserk.

Playing in 172 games, Joltin' Joe whacked out 270 base hits, slammed 34 homers, and drove in 154 runs. His batting average was a spectacular .398, and he was the scourge of the Pacific Coast League. There was little doubt about where he'd be playing his baseball once the 1936 season opened.

DiMag was a shy twenty-one years old when he reported to the Yanks' training camp at St. Petersburg, Florida, for spring training. He was already at his full height of 6'2", and he weighed 190 pounds. His slightly stooped appearance made him stand out in a crowd, and many of the older Yanks began giving him the rookie treatment.

"Here comes the new Babe Ruth. He sure don't look like the Babe," said one of his new teammates.

"Listen, kid," said another. "If you can hit .398 in the Pacific Coast League, you should hit at least .400 here. We have nice new white baseballs to swing at."

But once the season started, the kidding stopped. Actually, Joe was on the injured list until May 3. He had stayed under a heat lamp too long and burned an ankle. But when he was ready to go, the Yanks advertised his debut and 25,000 fans showed up to see this young man touted as the replacement for the Babe.

When Joe grounded out in his first at-bat, a voice hurtled from the boxes behind first base.

Some Babe!

It didn't faze Joe. The next time up he slammed a long triple off lefty Elon Hogsett. A pair of singles followed, and the Clipper had started his Yankee career with three hits.

Joe D. handled himself like a pro from the first. He was always a graceful outfielder who covered a lot of ground with his long, loping strides. His arm was strong and accurate. And if there was ever a question about his ability to hit major league pitching, he quickly dispelled that notion, too.

In his second game, he repeated his three-hit performance, then banged out another pair in the third contest. He kept up the pace and starred in the field. By mid-June, he was established. One day, Manager McCarthy called the Clipper into his office.

"Joe, we've just traded Chapman to Washington," the veteran skipper said. "From now on, you're the Yankee center-fielder."

The move showed how much confidence the Bombers had in their rookie. He didn't disappoint. When the season ended, Joe was batting .323, with 206 hits, 29 homers, and 125 runs batted in. What's more, he'd get a chance to appear in the World Series. The pennant-winning Yankees would be facing their old rivals, the New York Giants.

If Joe had a case of jitters, it never showed. He performed like a seasoned veteran in that pressure-packed Series. The Yanks won it in six games, with Joe D. a .346 hitter. He collected nine hits and drove in three runs. In addition, he showed the New Yorkers just what kind of an outfielder he was with a great running catch in deep center at the old Polo Grounds.

In fact, Joe himself was very pleased with his first season in the big leagues.

"I was a very satisfied young man," were the words he used in recalling that first season. "I played well, was with a wonderful bunch of fellows, and we won the pennant and World Series. What else could I ask for?"

That was a question on the minds of Yankee fans. What else? Would the young man from San Francisco turn out to be the next great Yankee superstar, or was he a flash in the pan?

It didn't take long to find out. As soon as the 1937 season opened, Joltin' Joe went to work. He was better than ever. Hit followed hit, homer followed homer, RBI piled on top of RBI. When it was over, the Yanks had won another pennant and their young centerfielder had a truly super season.

Joe played in 151 games that year, had 215 hits, slammed 46 homers to lead the league, and drove in 167 runs. He also led the league in runs scored with 151, and had a batting average of .346. In the Series, the Yanks topped the Giants in five games, and DiMag belted his first homer in the fall classic.

The next season, Joe got into a salary dispute with General Manager Ed Barrow, asking for $45,000 after receiving just $15,000 his second year. Barrow laughed, and reminded Joe that the great Lou Gehrig was only making $41,000. DiMag, never an outspoken or argumentive man, stammered for a minute, then replied:

"Mr. Barrow, Lou Gehrig is grossly underpaid!"

Barrow blew his stack. A stalemate developed, and Joe was a holdout when the season began. He missed the first two weeks, then settled for $25,000.

Pay scales were very different in those days. Joe hit .324 that year, with 32 homers and 140 RBI's. It was considered an off-year and he got a "token" hike to $27,000 the next season. In today's game, after a season like that, a young player would be demanding a $100,000 contract . . . and he'd have a chance of getting it.

A new pattern developed during the 1939 season that was to follow Joe for the rest of his career. Injuries! Shortly after the season started he tore muscles in his right leg and missed more than thirty games. When he returned, he hit like a man possessed, spraying the ball to all fields, and clouting deep shots into the leftfield stands.

With three weeks remaining in the season, the Yanks had clinched their fourth straight pennant and DiMag was batting .412. Then, it happened again. Joe began having trouble with a nerve in his eyelid. He didn't know what to do.

"Joe, you could sit out the next couple of weeks and hope the thing improves," Manager McCarthy said. "We've already won the pennant, so that's taken care of. But, remember, if you sit down now everyone will say we did it just to make you a .400 hitter. It's up to you."

Characteristically, Joe played. He didn't want to achieve something through the back door. The eye continued to bother him and his average dropped to .381. But it was still good enough for the batting title and enough to earn him the American League's Most Valuable Player Award. He also had 30 homers and 126 RBI's in just 120 games.

He added another homer in the Series, as the Yanks became the first team to win four world championships in a row. It took just four games for the Bombers to dispatch the Cincinnati Redlegs.

It was certainly a year of mixed emotions, with the injuries tempering what might have been a .400 season, perhaps his best ever. And it was also a year in which Lou Gehrig retired, suffering with the illness that was to cost him his life. But Joe married in 1939, an actress named Dorothy Arnold, and he was now the Yankee leader, the top gun on an outstanding team.

By 1941, the Yankee Clipper was an established veteran superstar. Both his brothers, Vince and Dom, were playing in the majors, and the Clipper had a son, Joe, Jr. It was also the year of his fabulous 56-game hitting streak, another Yankee pennant, and his second Most Valuable Player Award. But things would soon change for Joe, and for a lot of major leaguers.

Joe was twenty-eight years old when the 1942 season rolled around. He was a six-year veteran and at the peak of his career. But the nation was at war, and many of the top ballplayers enlisted. Joe completed the season, playing the entire schedule. It was an off-year. He hit just .305, with 21 homers and 114 RBI's. He looked forward to regaining his old form, but that would have to wait. The war was more important.

For three years, Joe played a lot of service ball, entertaining troops in America and in the Pacific. Joe's popularity was so great that this was the best way for him to contribute. It let the soldiers see, talk with, and play ball alongside the great Joe DiMaggio. He was happy to serve his country, but admitted that the three years had seemed like an eternity.

"I thought it would go on forever," he said. "Each year seemed more like ten."

It wasn't the happiest of times. When he returned for the 1946 season, his marriage had broken up, he was thirty-one years old, and hadn't played professional baseball for three years. It wouldn't be easy to get back in the groove. Some say he never really did.

Perhaps it was injuries, perhaps losing the peak years was too much. He hit just .290 in 132 games that first year back. Then, in 1947, he led the Yanks to a pennant with a .315 average, 20 homers, and 97 RBI's. It brought him his third MVP Award, but as Joe himself said:

"It wasn't the same that year. We won and I was MVP, but I knew I wasn't producing the same kind of season that I'd had so often before the war. I wondered if it would ever be the same."

It wouldn't. Not really. During the 1946 season, a bone spur on his left heel bothered him periodically. He had minor surgery to correct it during the off-season. In 1948, a worse spur developed on the right heel.

"Whenever I took a step it felt as if an ice pick was being driven into my heel."

Playing with pain, Joe nevertheless managed his best season since 1941. He missed just one game despite the spur and hit

.320, with league leading totals of 39 homers and 155 RBI's.

The spur grew worse. Surgery was necessary. It didn't work. He was in and out of the hospital in '49 and played in just seventy-six games. He still hit .346 with 14 homers and 67 RBI's, but the season was a disaster. Many fans thought he was through.

It took almost until June of 1950 before the pain left his foot. Joe worked to get back in shape, then returned to the lineup for a last hurrah. It came in the form of a .301 season, with 32 homers and 122 RBI's. He also clipped a homer in the World Series sweep of the Phillies.

But the next year it became obvious that most of the bounce had gone out of the Clipper. At thirty-seven, he had to struggle. He was visibly slowed at the plate and in the field. The layoff and nagging injuries had taken their toll. He hit just .263, with 12 homers and 71 RBI's in 116 games. It was obvious that he could no longer cut the mustard. In the Series, he managed six hits, including a homer and double, but he wasn't kidding himself.

"Baseball is no longer a game for me," he said shortly after the Yanks had won another championship. "It's become a struggle. I can't do what I used to on the field, and I'm not happy playing sub-par ball. I don't want to hang on. I've played my last game."

That was it. As dramatically as it began, the DiMaggio era had come to an end. There was a young rookie named Mantle with the team during the 1951 season, and perhaps Joe saw in him the continuation of the dynasty. He knew it was time to quit.

With three years lost to the war, and time out of the lineup because of injuries, Joe's lifetime totals aren't as impressive as some of the other greats of the game. For instance, he collected just 2,214 hits in his career, not nearly approaching the magic 3,000 figure. But he had a lifetime average of .325 and smacked out 361 homers. That figure, too, is well below the leaders, but he did well considering that right-handed batters traditionally have trouble hitting homers at Yankee Stadium.

But there was little doubt that the Yankee Clipper belonged up there with the great ones. Despite his early-career salary hassles, the Yankee front office showed its appreciation after the war, elevating him to the $70,000 class, then to the magical $100,000 circle for his final seasons.

The respect and reverence for Joe DiMaggio was evident during his retirement years. His number "5" was retired, to go alongside Babe Ruth's "3" and Lou Gehrig's "4" as Yankee numerals never to be worn again. When he donned his uniform for old timers' games at the Stadium, the cheers were the longest and loudest for the Clipper. And on several occasions when he put the ball in the seats during his one at-bat, the fans really went berserk. He was still their beloved Joe D.

The years were kind to Joe. He stayed slim, his hair grayed at the temples, and his handsome face took on a rather distinguished look.

A few years after his retirement, Joe shocked the sports world when he married actress Marilyn Monroe, a blonde bombshell at the zenith of her popularity. Joe was nearly forty, Miss Monroe twenty-seven. They met on a blind date, and she said she never even knew he was a ballplayer.

Unfortunately, the marriage lasted less than a year. Marilyn Monroe was in constant demand, she had so many commitments that she couldn't keep up with them. Joe was enjoying the first years of his retirement, and not really maintaining a busy schedule. It was just the wrong time for them.

Yet when Miss Monroe died prematurely several years later, it was Joe who stepped in and kept the funeral from becoming a Hollywood publicity extravaganza. The Yankee Clipper took over and gave his ex-wife a dignified farewell. His love and loyalty ran very deep.

Though he occasionally returned to the Yankees as a special batting instructor in spring training, Hall of Famer DiMaggio became a coach and vice-president of the Oakland Athletics. Owner Charles O. Finley was certainly capitalizing on the DiMaggio name, but Joe handled the job with his usual style and grace.

Even today, when Joe makes an appearance at old-timers' and charity games, it's not hard to envision him in his prime. A tremendously graceful ballplayer who made everything look easy, Joe DiMaggio was a standout performer and personality on a great baseball team. Had circumstances and injuries not caused him to lose so much time, his achievements would have been even greater.

His contemporaries knew it, too. When baseball held its centennial celebration in 1969, Joe DiMaggio was voted the game's Greatest Living Player. Quite an honor for a poor fisherman's son who grew up to become the Yankee Clipper.

THEODORE SAMUEL WILLIAMS

The Splendid Splinter

[1918–   ]

WHEN TED WILLIAMS reported to the Boston Red Sox training camp in the spring of 1938, he was so tall and skinny that they couldn't find a uniform to fit him properly. So when he trotted onto the field that first day, his too-short uniform shirt kept slipping out of his trousers.

Taking a quick look at the raw rookie, grizzly Manager Joe Cronin growled:

"Hey, busher. Stick in that shirttail. You're in the big leagues now!"

Williams returned his manager's scowl, made a fast dab at his shirttail, and continued on his way. No one had to tell Ted Williams that this was the big leagues. He knew it. It was the place he had always wanted to be. And no one had to tell Ted Williams what to do in the big leagues. He was ready. Even as a kid he once told one of his teachers, "Some day I'm gonna build a ballpark, put up cardboard fences, then knock 'em all down with home runs."

None of the fences in the big leagues were made of cardboard, but Theodore Samuel Williams did a pretty good job of knocking them down during his 23-year career, which was twice interrupted by war, and several times by disabling injury. Williams missed the better part of five seasons, his peak years, and still compiled a batting record envied by all but a select few.

Ted Williams could hit, all right. He could hit in his sleep, hit blindfolded, hit with the bat behind his back. He studied the art, practiced it, and then practiced it some more. Asked about present-day hitters recently, Williams looked up contemptuously.

"These kids don't know what practice means," he said flatly. "Hitting a baseball is the most difficult skill to master in all of sports. I'd spend every second hitting that I could. If I couldn't get someone to pitch to me, then I'd use the machine. But I'd keep swinging the bat, swinging the bat. Today, they take it all for granted."

No one ever took Ted Williams for granted, not when he had a hunk of Louisville Slugger in his hands.

Item. Young Ted Williams, just twenty years old, breaks into the Red Sox lineup and hits .327, with 31 homers and a league-leading 145 RBI's.

Item. Ted Williams, age twenty-two, becomes a .400 hitter with a sensational .406 season in 1941. He does it with six hits on the final day of the season. No batter has achieved that milestone since.

Item. Williams returns to the Red Sox in 1946 after three years of military duty and leads the team to a pennant with a .342 average, 38 home runs, and 123 RBI's.

Item. Recalled to service in Korea, Williams flies combat missions and almost loses his life in a crash-landing. Out of baseball for 15 months, he takes ten days of batting practice, then hits .407 in 37 games, with 13 homers and 34 RBI's in just 91 at bats.

Item. Ted Williams, at thirty-nine years of age, becomes

the oldest batting champion in baseball history with a .388 batting average in 1957.

Item. Announcing his retirement in 1960 at the age of forty-two, the Splendid Splinter steps to the plate for the last time and promptly cracks a long home run, the 521st of his career.

When the Splinter finally said good-by, he left behind a .344 lifetime batting average, 2,654 base hits, 521 homers, and 1,839 runs batted in. And that's with at least five peak years spent in service to his country.

But that's not all Williams left behind. A proud and stubborn man, the six-four, 200-pounder from San Diego, California, spent his career feuding with newsmen and fans. Highly sensitive, he couldn't handle the hyper-critical Boston press. He often refused interviews, sometimes spat at the press box in contempt, and let visiting writers know what he thought about the hometown scribes.

When the Fenway Park fans booed him for making an error and striking out one day in 1940, his second year, he vowed never again to tip his cap in appreciation of their applause. And though he heard plenty of cheers in the next two decades, he never as much as moved his hand near the brim of the cap. It is said that his hearing was so acute that he could pick out one or two jeers amidst the cheers of 30,000 fans.

If his ears were good, his eyes were even better. Stories about his vision are legendary. He once took a look at home plate in Fenway and informed the ground crew that it wasn't even. They didn't believe it, but a careful measurement showed it was off-center by a fraction.

His sense of touch was as highly developed, especially when it came to bats. He picked and chose with care, and he watched his bats like a hawk, making sure they didn't get wet or chewed up. He didn't want to alter the fine balance he achieved when he picked a war club.

One time, a bat manufacturer put five bats alongside one another and asked Ted to pick the one that was half an ounce heavier. Blindfolded, Ted carefully felt all the bats.

"This one," he said, holding out one of the clubs.

They scrambled the bats and he tried again. Once more, he chose the heavy bat, and both times he had been right. The manufacturer was amazed. Ted wasn't.

When he was batting, Ted was a picture of relaxed concentration. Standing midway in the batter's box, the left-hand-hitting Williams was loose, very loose. You could see the jangled movements as he got ready. But when the pitcher got set, all Ted's movement stopped and he stared out at the mound. Only his hands moved, grinding the handle of the bat, as if they couldn't wait to get at that baseball.

He had fast hands and wrists, and could whip the bat around in a flash. His speed allowed him to wait on a pitch a fraction longer than most, enabling him to "see" it better.

He was a tremendously coordinated hitter who looked as if he'd been born in a batter's box. He almost defied pitchers to throw at him, planting his left foot solidly and never moving it. He'd just lean out of the way of close pitches. Hitting Williams wouldn't serve any useful purpose. It would just make him madder.

Then there came the "Williams shift." It was started in 1946 by Cleveland's player-manager Lou Boudreau. Angered because Williams had been murdering the Indians with his bat, Boudreau stationed three men on the right side of the infield when Ted came to bat. Only the third baseman remained on the left side. Boudreau gambled that Ted's pride would make him try to beat the shift instead of punching the ball to left.

Williams steamed when he saw it. He roared his disgust and promptly hit a home run to win the game.

But the shift bothered him. Boudreau was right. Ted didn't want to bunt or push the ball to left. He continued to swing away against the shift and lost more than a few base hits whenever it was used over the years.

Always his own man, Ted said what he pleased and did what he wanted. He hated to wear ties, and took to wearing open-necked shirts in an age when few did it. Things like that never mattered to the Splinter.

He was always steeped in some kind of controversy. When they picked on his defensive play (which was somewhat less than the best), he'd answer, "I make my money with my bat, not my glove," and proceed to prove it the next time up. In all fairness, he did become a competent outfielder later in his career, though he was never a real speed merchant on the picket line.

No matter how you slice the pie, hitting was what Ted Williams did best. And he'd been doing that for a long time.

The Splendid Splinter was California-born, on August 30, 1918. He didn't have a really happy childhood. His father was something of a wanderer, and his mother spent much of her time working for the Salvation Army. So young Ted took to baseball. It gave him something to do and provided companionship. But he played more often and stayed longer than any of the other boys. It was obvious that he was already practicing, not just playing a casual game.

When he attended Herbert Hoover High School in San Diego, he was already a star hitter, but the rest of his game —running and fielding—was sorely lacking. Still, when he finished his high-school days, he was a .430 career hitter, a pretty fair pitcher, and an average outfielder.

Shortly after graduating from high school, Ted signed with San Diego of the Pacific Coast League for $150 per month. He was just seventeen years old, skinny as a rail though he ate like a horse.

He was also a shy youth and a nervous wreck when he pinch hit the first time and took three called strikes. But it wasn't long before the base hits started falling in. He hit just .271 that first year, 1936, but came to bat only 107 times. Ironically, he showed no promise as a power hitter, failing to hit a single home run and driving home just 11 runs. The next year was better. He gained weight during the off-season and raised his average to .291, with 23 homers and 98 RBI's.

That's when the Red Sox bought him, offering the nineteen year old a two-year contract at $3,000; then $4,500. At the urging of his parents, the Splinter held out for a $1,000 bonus, and got it. Then he went to work. Assigned to Minneapolis of the American Association, Ted promptly won the triple crown with a .366 average, 43 homers, and 142 RBI's. It wasn't surprising.

Ted had trained with the Sox that year, and three of the vets needled the brash youngster when he was sent to the minors. The Splinter snarled back.

"You tell them something for me," he told his friend, clubhouse man Johnny Orlando. "Tell those wise guys that I'll be back and I'm gonna make more money out of this game than all three of them put together ever did."

Then he went to Minnesota and began proving his point. He didn't get along with his manager, Donie Bush, but there was no way his batting feats could be ignored. The Sox weren't about to let this tall package of base hits get away.

When the 1939 season opened, Ted was in right field for the Red Sox. He proceeded to tear the league apart, leading the junior circuit in RBI's with 145, a record for a rookie, and his .327 batting average was nothing to scoff at. Even the great Babe Ruth marveled at the young phenom.

"He's the Rookie of the Year in my book," said the Babe. "Best young hitter I've seen in a long time."

Ted didn't stop. He was up to .344 the next season, though his homer and RBI totals fell off somewhat (23, 113). Then came the 1941 season and Ted really took off.

He was over the .400 mark for the entire season. That was the same year Joe DiMaggio had his fabulous 56 game hit streak. Joe batted .408 during the streak, but Ted always liked to point out that he batted .412 over that same period of time, and he didn't have a streak going.

Anyway, on the final day of the season, the Sox had a doubleheader with Philadelphia, and Ted's average was .399955. That close. Manager Cronin came up to him before the first game.

"Ted, you don't have to play today if you don't want to. Your average will be recorded as .400."

"Nothing doing," snapped the Kid. "No one's gonna say Ted Williams made .400 by his shoestrings. Count me in."

When he came up for the first time, the A's catcher, Frank Hayes, said, "Listen, Ted, Mack (Manager Connie Mack) told us if we let up on you he'll run us off the team. You won't get any gifts today."

"I don't want any," answered Williams, and he dug in at the plate.

Batting against righty Dick Fowler, Ted slammed a single. He could have called it a day right there. He was officially over .400. But he didn't. Next time up he slammed a long homer. Again, he refused to come out. Two more singles followed. Surely, he'd call it a day now?

"Put me in the second game," he told Cronin bluntly. "I'm not through yet."

He wasn't. He doubled and singled in the second game and ended up with a six-for-eight day and a .406 average. Ted Williams had become a .400 hitter by a little more than his shoestrings.

Still, the big news that year was DiMaggio's hit streak, and the Yankee Clipper won the League's Most Valuable Player Award.

An angered Ted came back the next season and won the triple crown, hitting .356, banging out 36 homers, and driving home 137 runs. He didn't win the MVP again. That went to Joe Gordon, who hit just .322.

Ted had been having some difficulties with the draft board, being deferred to support his mother, and he thought that this might have figured in the MVP voting. He finally went into the service after the 1942 season, and although he saw no action he was a combat-ready Marine pilot when he was discharged.

The long layoff hurt many ballplayers. Not Williams. He could hit in his sleep. Boston won the pennant that year and Ted finally got the MVP Award.

Ted had a bad time in his only World Series. The Cardinal pitchers worked carefully to him and he managed just five singles and one RBI in twenty-five at-bats. The Sox lost, four games to three, and Ted was crushed. He blamed himself and wouldn't even keep his share of the winnings. He gave the money to Johnny Orlando.

His only consolation that year was the all-star game. He had four straight hits in the mid-season classic, including one of the strangest home runs he ever hit.

Ted was facing Rip Sewell, a Pittsburgh righthander who threw a trick pitch called the "eephus." It was a high-arching blooper-ball that floated down over the plate from above. It was more entertainment than anything else, but Sewell got a charge out of watching batters fan the breeze at it. He'd like nothing better than to make the great Ted Williams look bad.

Sure enough, Sewell threw the eephus. But Ted was ready. He took two quick steps forward, and got the ball before it dropped across the plate. There was the eephus, sailing high and deep over the right field wall and it was Ted who had the last laugh that time.

He continued his bashing, winning the triple crown for the second time in 1947. Then there was a .369 year in '48, and a second MVP award in '49. That year he hit .343, belted a career high of forty-three homers with 159 RBI's.

A broken elbow in the 1950 all-star game limited him to eighty-nine contests that year. The next season his average dipped to .318, but he managed 30 homers and 126 RBI's. This was also the high point of his feud with the Boston press and fans. He didn't like the way they treated him and he let them know about it.

Then came Korea and suddenly Ted found himself a fighter pilot. He played in six games that year, then left for the war. A crash landing almost cost him his life and left his hearing slightly impaired, but he came back near the end of the 1953 season. He thought about retirement, but Branch Rickey, the grand Mahatma of baseball, talked him into continuing.

"You can hit better than any of these kids," Rickey said. "Get out there and show them how it's done."

The next years Ted was up to his usual tricks. Though slowed by a variety of injuries, he put together seasons of .345, .356, and .345, although his homer and RBI totals dipped somewhat.

Then came the 1957 season. Ted was thirty-nine years old, and many writers predicted that he'd lose it that year. Well, if anything, he got it back. Playing in 132 games, he batted an amazing .388, to become the oldest man ever to win the batting title. He also smacked out thirty-eight homers and drove home eighty-seven runs. During the second half of the season, Ted batted an incredible .453, yet he lost still another MVP prize, this time to Mickey Mantle, who was second to him with a .365 average.

To show it was no freak, he won his seventh and final batting crown the next year, hitting a crisp .328. Then, in 1959, he had the only "off" year of his career. Bothered by a neck injury that wouldn't get well, he batted just .254 in 103 games. They said he was through. When asked about retirement, he growled:

"I'm not going out like that."

So he came back for a last fling at age forty-two in 1960. And he showed he could still hit the baseball. Coming to the plate 310 times, Ted Williams batted .316, banged out 29 more home runs, and drove home 72 runs. He still had the batting eye, but everything else was too hard. It was time to go, and he made the announcement even before the season ended, bowing out with a dramatic home run before the home fans. And for one final time, Ted Williams refused to tip his cap, despite a thunderous ovation.

Ted Williams has always been his own man. Elected to the Hall of Fame the first time he was eligible, Ted addressed the writers who voted, many of whom he had feuded with throughout the years.

"I can't really say I've got a lot of close friends out there," he said, smiling. "So I knew the people who voted for me did it because they feel in their minds and hearts that I must have deserved it. To them I say, thank you, from the bottom of my heart."

To close friends who knew him, that was the real Ted Williams. There was a warm spot for those he liked, and for youngsters. For years, he'd given his time and energy to help the Jimmy Fund, a child cancer fund in the Boston area. And one time, he chartered a plane to visit a boy in a Carolina hospital who had asked for Ted as he lay on his deathbed.

But he couldn't get away from trouble. Two marriages ended in divorce, the papers blowing the stories up each time.

Williams in retirement remained the sportsman. One of the best-known fisherman in America, Ted went into the equipment business, manufacturing fishing tackle and making many personal appearances in activities connected with the only other sport he ever loved.

In 1966, he returned to baseball when Bob Short, owner of the Washington Senators, persuaded him (with the help of a huge contract) to manage the Washington team. Most people thought Ted would lack patience, but he worked diligently with the young players, and, after one year, the team's regulars had improved their batting averages by almost twenty points a man.

Still, Short traded away good ballplayers and couldn't replace them from his farm system. The team floundered, and the novelty wore off. Ted hung on though, even when the team moved to Arlington, Texas, before the 1972 season. But that was the final straw. He resigned at the end of the season, saying it was time to do a little fishing.

Ted Williams once told a reporter that his favorite prize-fighter was Ezzard Charles, a former heavyweight champ who received little recognition from the public. When asked why, the Splinter answered:

"I like underrated people. You see in them more extraordinary qualities than in some of the heroes you worshipped."

That was Williams, all right. He never had an idol in his life, always preferring to go his own way. But no one . . . no one . . . ever dared underrate Ted Williams' ability to hit a baseball.

JACK ROOSEVELT ROBINSON
The Pioneer

[1919–1972]

It's easy to take baseball for granted. The game is part of the American scene. People today cheer their favorite stars at ballparks throughout the country, and they think about how they can hit and run, not about their color. Yet less than thirty years ago, men like Willie Mays, Henry Aaron, Dick Allen, Roberto Clemente, and Vida Blue weren't allowed to play in the major leagues.

Sometimes it seems incredible that it took so long for the national pastime to become truly national. But not until 1947 did a black man pull on the uniform of a big league team.

When it finally happened, the man who had been chosen to break the so-called color line was indeed an extraordinary human being. Otherwise, he'd never have survived his first season as a major leaguer.

That man was Jackie Robinson.

He came to the Brooklyn Dodgers as a 28-year-old rookie in 1947, with some of his best years already behind him. He'd spent those years in the Negro Leagues, where all blacks before him had had to play their baseball.

Despite poor playing conditions, low pay, very few fans, and next to no press coverage, Negro League legends grew.

Men like Satchel Paige and Josh Gibson were the Walter Johnsons and Babe Ruths of their leagues. All those who saw them in action said they would have been superplayers in the major leagues as well.

It wasn't until 1945 that one courageous baseball man felt the time had come for something to be done. His name was Branch Rickey, and he had just become president and general manager of the Brooklyn Dodgers. Rickey wanted the Brooks to be a powerhouse, and he knew he'd have to get the ballplayers to do it.

He went about restructuring the team's policies on signing young players, working them into the Dodger farm system. It was the same Rickey who, while at St. Louis, had devised the modern farm system, enabling a team to sign and train its own ballplayers. The system had worked very well and was used by many big league teams. Now Rickey had another idea. He told it to one of the Dodger executives.

"I want to sign a lot of kids, even fifteen and sixteen year olds. We've got to start now if we want to have a strong team in the next decade. We'll beat the bushes, dig these kids up wherever they're hiding. And who knows, we might even include a Negro player or two."

Rickey already knew what he wanted—a black player for the Dodgers. He was just being very careful how he broke the news of his idea to those around him. When he received favorable vibrations from the others in the Dodger front office, he set to work.

He told his scouts that he was thinking of organizing a new Negro League and he asked them to look at the present Negro teams for the best talent available. He wanted to know about all the top ballplayers on clubs like the Kansas City Monarchs and Indianapolis Clowns. But what Branch

Rickey was really looking for was one special kind of man.

When all the reports were in, Rickey called scout Clyde Sukeforth into his office.

"Tell me a little more about this Robinson fellow," he said.

"He's a good one," answered the veteran scout. "He can run, field, and hit . . . and he's smart. Plus he's a real fighter out there. I think he could play for any team in our league right now."

Rickey was interested. He checked Robinson's background, then sent for the young man, who was starring for the Kansas City Monarchs.

When Jackie entered Branch Rickey's office in late August of 1945, he was twenty-six years old. Thick of build, the young athlete stood just under six feet and weighed a solid two hundred pounds. He was wide through the chest and hips, right down to the legs. But Rickey knew he was a former trackman and could really move.

Jackie had a handsome, dark face with subdued features. He didn't smile much and viewed the older man from under a skeptical, raised brow. He spoke in a sharp, direct manner, in a voice high-pitched but sure of itself. Though he didn't know exactly what Rickey wanted, he certainly wasn't frightened or intimidated.

Then the cagey Rickey began to explain his plan, how he wanted Jackie to be the man to break the color line, to play major league baseball for the Brooklyn Dodgers. He said it wouldn't be easy, that many people, for a variety of reasons, would be slow to accept a black man in the majors.

"There will be virtually no one on our side," he told Jackie. "Not the owners, not the umpires, and very few newspapermen. Many fans are going to be hostile. We've got to convince everyone that this is right because you are a great ballplayer and a fine gentleman."

He told Jackie that he'd have to turn the other cheek in situations where he normally would react. Then Rickey dramatized some of the things Robby would run into, actually insulting the young athlete, calling him common, bigoted names, taunting him. Branch Rickey could see Jackie bristle with anger. He knew the black man was outspoken and a fighter. But he also knew he had a keen intelligence as well as the toughness not to fight back even when tempted.

Jackie admitted it would be difficult. But he had been through some rough times in his life up to then, and he wasn't about to back off, especially when there was so much at stake.

"I'm your man," said Jackie Robinson.

Jack Roosevelt Robinson was born on January 31, 1919, in Cairo, Georgia. His father and mother separated when he was one, and Mrs. Robinson took her five children to Pasadena, California, where she went to work as a servant in order to care for them. Little Jack tagged after his older sister as soon as he was old enough to walk.

Shortly after he started attending school himself, he discovered he was the best athlete in the class, and it paid off. The other kids were buying him lunch and giving him other things just so he'd play on their team.

"I was probably one of the youngest professionals ever," he once said, fondly remembering those early days.

Big-time sports came to the Robinson family early. Jackie's older brother, Mack, became a champion sprinter and finished second to the great Jesse Owens in the 200-meter dash at the 1936 Olympics. His ability gave young Jack a boost and made him look to a career in sports, too.

After graduating from high school, Jackie attended Pasadena Junior College, then went to UCLA in 1939. A scholarship paid part of his way, and he got odd jobs to earn the rest. But once at the California school, he made his mark in a hurry, becoming the first man to letter in all four major sports.

He starred as a halfback on the UClans football team, running for an average of twelve yards per carry and gaining more yardage than anyone in the country. When he switched to the basketball court, he quickly became the high scorer in the conference. In track, he broke the Pacific Coast League long jump record. As for baseball, he played second and was the star of the team. There didn't seem to be anything he couldn't do on an athletic field.

Although he was an outstanding ballplayer at UCLA, his classroom work was just mediocre. Jackie didn't enjoy studying, and soon indicated that he'd rather stay with athletics and perhaps coach then study for a profession. In fact, after playing four sports for two years, he left school without attaining his degree.

By the end of 1940, he was working for the National Youth Administration as an assistant athletic director. He got back into action the next year, playing football for the Los Angeles Bulldogs, a professional team.

When the war came, Jack enlisted and entered Officer's Candidates School. He was commissioned a lieutenant, but an old ankle injury prevented him from being sent overseas. He did get into one notable scrape, refusing to go to the back of the bus when ordered there by a bigoted driver. The incident went all the way to the court-martial stage before Jackie was cleared. He had stood up for his rights and won.

When he returned from the service, he coached briefly at

Samuel Houston College in Austin, Texas, then joined the Kansas City Monarchs as a shortstop for $400 a month. It wasn't long after that Jackie had his famous meeting with Branch Rickey.

There was one other thing that Rickey asked Jackie before he left that day.

"Do you have a girl, Jackie?" he asked.

"Yes, I do."

"Take my advice, son. Marry her."

Jackie took the advice. He'd been thinking of marrying Rachel Isum, whom he had met at UCLA, for some time. Little did he know that Rickey was just giving his usual advice. He thought a married ballplayer was more reliable and always suggested that his players tie the marital knot.

When the 1946 baseball season rolled around, Jackie was set to play for the Montreal Royals in the American Association. Montreal was the Dodgers' top farm club. Assigning Jackie to the Royals tipped the baseball world to exactly what Rickey had in mind. That's when Jackie's ordeal began.

Manager Clay Hopper was from Mississippi. Right away, he questioned Rickey's wisdom in giving Robinson to the Royals. But he couldn't question Jackie's ability, so he installed him at second base. Robby made $600 a month and, with a $3,500 bonus, the money wasn't bad. But he had to earn every penny of it.

Right from the start, there was bench jockeying. And the taunts at Robby had a tone all their own. They were usually slurred, with the color of his skin the regular target. Jackie tried to ignore them, but, being highly sensitive, he couldn't. He burned inside, but remembered his promise to Rickey. He turned the other cheek. The only place he could vent his anger was at bat and on the base paths.

Batting from the right side, he stood midway in the box and held his bat high and away from his body. He had a rather unique, stiff-armed swing, but he whacked hard line drives all over the field.

On the base paths he was greased lightning. He drove pitchers crazy, dancing and jiving off the bag, threatening to steal on every pitch. And when he did go, he usually made it.

He was also a good fielder. He came to Montreal as a shortstop, but didn't have the quick arm for the position. That's why they put him at second. Later, he was to show his versatility by playing first, second, third, and the outfield for the Dodgers.

But at Montreal, the great experiment seemed to be working. Jackie was standing up under tremendous pressure and playing outstanding baseball. He was successfully withstanding the constant taunts and knockdown pitches and responding with base hits.

The season reached a climax when Montreal played Louisville for the American Association championship. The series opened in Louisville, and that Kentucky city was up in arms about the black star of the Royals. There was a threat of racial conflict in the air, and only a small number of blacks were allowed into the ballpark. The white fans treated Jackie as if he were the devil himself.

They taunted him, threw things on the field, booed, and hissed every time he stepped to the plate. Whether Jackie was rattled or not is hard to say, but he didn't do well. When the team returned to Montreal, the fans greeted him like a long-lost hero, and took their wrath out on the visiting Louisville players.

Both Robby and the other Royals responded, playing great ball the rest of the way and winning the title. After the game, the Montreal fans wouldn't leave the field until Jackie came out. He was a hero to them. They appreciated his outstanding play and knew he'd be with the Dodgers next year. They wanted to say good-by and thank him.

"It was one of the most moving moments of my life," Jackie said later. "They were all over me, shaking my hand, slapping my back, and talking in French and English. Finally, I just had to run away. It's probably one of the few times a black man had to run from a white crowd for a reason other than them wanting to lynch him."

Manager Hopper owed Jackie a lot, too. Though he had been dubious of the move at first, the Montreal skipper told Branch Rickey:

"Don't worry about him. He's a fine athlete and he's gonna make it for you. And what's more, he's a gentleman."

It would be difficult to ignore a man who had just led the league in hitting with a .349 average and driven in sixty-six runs. That about clinched it. Rickey informed his young star that he'd be playing for the Dodgers in 1947.

Word spread around the majors like wildfire, and the flames of ignorance and bigotry were fanned in many big league cities. It started for Jackie and his wife in spring training, when it was difficult for them to find living quarters and places to eat. Some games had to be canceled because of the commotion caused by Jackie's playing in southern parks.

Then the team came north and opened the season against Philadelphia. Things didn't get much better. The Phils, led by manager Ben Chapman, let Jackie have it with both barrels, and it wasn't very nice. He almost went into the Philadelphia dugout with a baseball bat, and it took tremendous restraint for him to hold back.

Jackie was playing first base for the Dodgers, and two of

the other infielders, shortstop Pee Wee Reese and second baseman Eddie Stanky, were both southerners. Yet they knew what they'd have to do. Stanky returned the challenge to the Philly bench, and Reese calmly walked over at one point and draped his arm around Jackie's shoulder. At least the Dodgers were going to stick together.

That was pretty much the pattern the first year. There was some talk of a petition going around to get Jackie out of the league, but it never surfaced publicly. The heckling remained, and the inbred resentment, the result of a social pattern going back many years, was also still in evidence. But once Jackie had made a trip around the league and the initial novelty of the whole thing wore off, it was time to play baseball.

Jackie stayed at first base most of that year, playing in 151 games. It was a pennant season for the Dodgers and there was joy and wild jubilation in Brooklyn. The rookie's contribution to the win had been noticeable. Despite the constant pressure and humiliation, Jackie batted .297 in 1947, banging out 175 hits, 12 homers, and driving home 48 runs. He showed his speed and deception by leading the league with twenty-nine stolen bases. He was a definite asset to the team and was named Rookie of the Year by the *Sporting News*.

The World Series that year brought heartbreaking loss to the Yanks in seven games. But Jackie had seven hits and showed that the pressure didn't bother him one bit.

Jackie had a problem the next year, and it wasn't related to his usual one. It was his weight. He reported to camp at 230 pounds, almost thirty pounds more than he had weighed the year before. This slowed him up and it took him several months to get into top shape. He finished with an average of .296, and increased his RBI total to eighty-five. It hadn't made Rickey happy to see his long-time investment carrying all that heft. He told Jackie to slim down before the next season got underway.

Determined not to let Branch Rickey down, Jackie responded with a slimmer waistline and the greatest season of his career. He started with a bang and never stopped. At the plate he was deadly, spraying line drives all over the field, hitting with power and coming through in the clutch. On the bases, he was an elusive flash. When he wasn't stealing, he was a constant threat to steal, and he drove pitchers crazy with his base path antics.

Jackie was happier in the field in 1949. With Stanky gone, he was the new second baseman, and had a fine season at that position. The Dodgers were soon en route to another pennant, beating out the Cards with a September push led by Jackie and rightfielder Carl Furillo.

Robby's statistics for the year were eye-opening. He led the National League in hitting with a .342 average, slammed out 203 hits, belted 16 homers, and drove home 124 runs. He also led the loop in stolen bases with thirty-seven.

Although the Dodgers sustained another defeat in the Series, Jackie Robinson was named the National League's Most Valuable Player for the season.

By now, Jackie was no longer a national phenomenon. The first year had been the tough one. Now there were more black ballplayers coming into the league. Roy Campanella had joined the Dodgers in 1948, Monte Irvin was playing with the Giants, Larry Doby was making his presence felt with the Indians in the American League. It wouldn't be long before others like Willie Mays were arriving on the scene. Times were changing. Some teams were slower to yield than others, but the necessity of winning made it imperative for teams to take the talent available and not worry about color any more.

Jackie's role had also changed. That first year, he had had to be especially careful. He knew there'd be people trying to run him out of the league. Now he was there to stay. He could open up more, begin to make his feelings known. Always an intelligent, articulate spokesman for the rights of minorities, once he got into high gear there was no stopping him.

Pretty soon, he had a reputation as a controversial and outspoken figure. Appearing on a television show, he was asked if he thought the Yankees discriminated against blacks.

"Yes," answered Jackie without hesitation, starting a citywide row that lasted several weeks. Whenever reporters were looking for some good copy, they came to Jackie.

On the field, he was part of the Brooklyn baseball dynasty of the late forties and early fifties. The Dodgers won pennants in '47, '49, '52, and '53, but lost to the Yanks in the World Series each time. Yet the team was great. Gil Hodges, Duke Snider, Pee Wee Reese, Roy Campanella, Billy Cox, Carl Furillo, Preacher Roe, Don Newcombe, and Jackie were all fine ballplayers.

It was a power team, all right, and tiny Ebbets Field was a perfect place for the Dodgers to play. The home runs flew out of the park with regularity. Because of all the Dodger sluggers, Jackie didn't have to run the bases as much as he would have liked. Yet he remained one of the most feared runners in the league.

And he continued to produce at the plate. His batting averages from 1950 to 1954 were .328, .338, .308, .329, and .311. There was no doubt that he was a genuine star player in the National League.

By 1955, Jackie was thirty-six years old and beginning to slow down. The Dodgers were spotting him at different positions now. He wasn't playing every day and it was obvious that he didn't have much time left.

His contribution to the 1955 pennant wasn't as great as it had been in the past. He slumped to a career-low of .256 and drove in just thirty-six runs. But this time the Dodgers finally turned the tables on the Yanks and won the World Series in seven games. Jackie played in six of the contests and hit just .182, but he excited the crowd by stealing home in the first game. He was on a world championship team at last.

He came back for one more year in 1956, batted .275 in 117 games, then called it a career. He just didn't have the legs any more, and running was a big part of his game. Another thing that prompted his decision was a trade the Dodgers proposed that had him going to the Giants. He'd have none of that.

Jackie only played in the majors for ten years. But he compiled a lifetime average of .311, and had he had the time for a full career, he would have undoubtedly set some outstanding records. Just recently, a sportswriter put that very fact in a clearer perspective.

"Robinson was the most aggressively exciting player of my experience," the writer said. "Ty Cobb was before my time, but I saw Babe Ruth and DiMaggio, Musial and Willie Mays, Aaron and Ted Williams. Robinson's statistical record seems meager compared with theirs, but if all of them were somehow playing on the same team I have no doubt that Robinson would be the dominating figure. He made things happen. He was an extraordinary man."

That's what the Hall of Fame committee thought, too. They voted Jackie in the first time he was eligible in 1962.

"Maybe I shouldn't have been the guy Mr. Rickey chose to be first," Jackie once said. "I had to store a lot of stuff in me those first couple of years. After that, I decided to talk when I had something to say. I think I played better that way."

Branch Rickey agreed, playing down his own role in Jackie's success. "All the credit belongs to Jackie," Rickey said. "He's the one who put up with all the abuse, turned the other cheek when he had to, and became a great ballplayer."

Life was never easy for Jackie Robinson. He, Rachel, and their three children moved into a large home in Stamford, Connecticut, and, once his playing days were over, he took a vice-president's job with a large restaurant chain. But wherever Jackie went, trouble always seemed to be lurking nearby. He was either speaking up on a controversial issue or running into some personal misfortune.

He left his corporate job in 1964, to become involved in banking, social problems, and politics. He kept a busy schedule, and his health began to fail. He contracted diabetes, had a mild heart attack, and eventually lost the sight in one eye. When his oldest son, Jack, Jr., was killed in an automobile accident after serving in Vietnam and successfully battling a drug problem, it was a bitter blow to the white-haired father.

His last public appearance was at the 1972 World Series. Speaking before a huge crowd, Jackie jumped into the fray once more.

"I'm proud to be here," he said in his clear voice. "But I'll be even more proud when I look over at the third base dugout and see a black man managing in the major leagues."

It was one dream Jackie wouldn't get to see. On the morning of the following October 24, he suffered a heart attack at his Stamford home and died instantly.

The sports world was shocked, and the eulogies poured in.

It was only then that people were reminded of the great contribution Jackie Robinson had made to his country and to his race.

Perhaps his impact might best be noted by a return to a happier event of 1972. *Sport* magazine, celebrating a quarter of a century of publishing, decided to honor the best performers from each sport over that period of time. In addition, there was one special, overriding award given to the athlete designated as "Man of the 25 Years." No one disputed the choice. It was Jackie Robinson.

All the greats from the sports world were there to honor the old Dodger. Jackie was deeply touched that night, and when he spoke, he said simply:

"This great honor says to me that a man can be acclaimed for standing up to his convictions."

Then there were tributes by others in attendance. "Not many people could have gone through what he had to," his old friend Pee Wee Reese said.

"He's the man I've cursed, hated, cheered, rooted for, and idolized," was the comment made by former Giant rival Monte Irvin.

But it was probably former basketball great Bill Russell who said it best. Russell is a man from another sport, another era; yet Jackie Robinson had a tremendous impact on his life.

"You have no idea what Jackie Robinson has meant to me," said Russell. "He's a man who played baseball—on a Hall of Fame level—under the worst circumstances. He did it without losing his manhood or his humanness. That's really extraordinary. I'd go around the world to honor him. He's one of the men I've admired all my life."

Jack Roosevelt Robinson should be admired. He was one of the great pioneers of our time.

STANLEY FRANK MUSIAL

The Man

[1 9 2 0 –   ]

IT WAS A LAZY August afternoon in 1940. The Daytona Beach team of the Florida State League was playing at Orlando. It was a close game, Daytona leading by a run, but the home team had men on second and third, and their top hitter was coming up.

In centerfield for Daytona, a nineteen-year-old youngster named Stan Musial took a few steps to his right.

"This guy pulls a lot into the gap," he thought. "Got to be ready."

Musial knew about the Florida State hitters for two reasons. First of all, he had watched them from his outfield position. He played 113 games on the picket line for Daytona Beach, and showed great promise as a hitter, with a .311 batting average in 405 trips to the plate. He had driven in seventy runs with the aid of just one homer.

But there was another reason Stan Musial knew the hitters. He had pitched to most of them. Stan Musial was a regular starting pitcher for Daytona that year, as well as playing the outfield. On the mound he compiled an impressive, 18–5 record in 223 innings. The fast-balling lefthander fanned 176 batters and had an earned-run average of 2.62.

"I don't know, Stan," Daytona Manager Dickie Kerr had often said, "whether you'll make it to the majors as a pitcher or a hitter. But I do know one thing. You'll make it."

Stan smiled to himself, remembering the confidence Dickie Kerr had in him. Then, with the pitcher getting set to throw, Stan concentrated on the game.

He saw the bat flash, and immediately began running to his right. Sure enough, the big guy had sent one into the left centerfield gap.

"If it drops in, they win the game," Stan thought, as he ran as hard as he could. "I've got to catch it."

He saw it was going to be a close play. Straining every muscle, he dove for the sinking liner, and felt it catch in the webbing of his glove before he hit the ground.

From the dugout, Manager Kerr saw Stan make the catch, then watched him tumble in a complete somersault, still holding the ball.

"Out!" hollered the umpire, and the side was retired.

The Daytona players began trotting into the dugout, buzzing about Stan's catch, but when they turned to congratulate him, they saw him still sprawled on the outfield grass, clutching at his left shoulder.

"I'm all right, I'm all right . . . just a little dazed," Stan insisted as they helped him to his feet and off the field. "Don't worry, I'll be able to pitch tomorrow."

But as soon as he removed his baseball shirt and saw the big lump on his shoulder, he knew he wouldn't be all right by the next day. In fact, the arm would never be all right again, at least as far as his pitching was concerned.

Stan didn't realize it right away, but when he thought the arm was healed and tried to pitch, he quickly came to a conclusion.

"My arm's dead," he told Dickie Kerr. "I'm through."

"Hey, come on, Stan," his manager and good friend said. "Maybe your pitching days are numbered, but I think you can make the grade as a hitter. From now on, you're my regular leftfielder. And I'll bet you won't be here for long."

Dickie Kerr was right. As soon as he began to concentrate on hitting full time, Stan Musial began to think he could make it. He was with three clubs the next season: Springfield, Rochester, and the St. Louis Cardinals. And when he got to the Cards, he was there to stay . . . for twenty-three seasons, to be exact. Although he didn't know it then, Stan "The Man" Musial was about to become a legend in his own time.

Before he hung up his spikes, Stanley Frank Musial was destined to play more games and get more base hits than any man with the exception of the great Ty Cobb. There was no one ahead of Stan when it came to total bases and most long hits. He got more than anyone. The list of records that Stan holds or shares is endless.

He was a mainstay of the St. Louis Cardinals for more than twenty years. He had a lifetime batting average of .331, belted 475 home runs, and drove 1,951 runs across the plate. A versatile, clutch performer, Stan is the only player in major league history to have played more than one thousand games as an infielder, and one thousand games as an outfielder.

And through it all, he was a modest, easy-going, team player, showing none of the temperamental quirks that often characterize superstars. He just liked to play ball. As long as he could come to the plate and hit, he was happy.

It was easy to tell when Stan was hitting. He had one of the most unusual batting stances ever. A lefthander all the way, Stan would set himself midway in the box, feet close together. He'd then bend at the knees, leaning over slightly, and turning his head toward the pitcher. The bat was held near his left shoulder, very still, almost straight in the air. One writer once said Stan looked like a kid peeking around a corner when he hit.

But how he could hit! Exploding out of the stance with a quick, level swing and classic follow-through, Stan hit line drives to all fields. Singles, doubles, triples, homers . . . it didn't matter. Stan hit them all. Never considered a real power hitter, he nevertheless managed close to five hundred home runs. On ten different occasions he drove in one hundred or more runs in a season. He had more doubles (725) than any man in history other than Tris Speaker. And he led the National League in hitting seven times.

He was a three-time Most Valuable Player, was named Player of the Decade by the *Sporting News* in 1956, and was elected to the Hall of Fame in 1969, the first year he was eligible. It was the fans in Brooklyn, as critical as they come, who gave him his nickname. He was simply "The Man." That's how good they thought he was.

But even Stan the Man was a boy once, and that boyhood was spent in Donora, Pennsylvania, where he was born on November 21, 1920. He was the fifth of six children born to Mary and Lukasz Musial. His father was a Polish immigrant who came to America to start a new life. He settled in Donora and found employment in a wire mill. Mr. Musial worked very hard, and at one point earned just eleven dollars every two weeks. So life was not easy for the family.

In fact, when Stan first started playing ball as a youngster, his mother made him a ball by sewing together scraps of material she had around the house because they couldn't afford the price of a real one.

Young Stan had dreams of being a ballplayer from the time he was eight years old. One of his neighbors, a man named Joe Barboa, had been a minor leaguer at one time. He managed the local team and talked a lot of baseball to Stan and his brother, while they played catch with them in his yard. Stan heard stories of many famous ballplayers and their dynamic deeds on the diamond, and he dreamed of being just like them some day.

When he was about fifteen, his arm was already strong enough for him to pitch against grown men. Playing a local team one afternoon, he struck out thirteen men in six innings.

Playing against boys his own age, he was even better, and by the time he got to high school, he was a star in both basketball and baseball. In fact, his high-school coach thought Stan was such a natural athlete that he wanted him to play football to increase his chances for an athletic scholarship to college. Stan refused.

By the time he was a junior in 1937, he was coming to a major decision in his life. He had tried out with the Cardinals at their area farm club, and he wanted to turn pro. More than anything else, he wanted to be a baseball player.

But his parents had other ideas, especially his father. Mr. Musial knew the disadvantages of not having an education. He desperately wanted his son to attend college.

"Your coach tells me you have a good chance to get a basketball scholarship," the father said one night at dinner.

Stan just bowed his head.

"Well, speak up, Stashu," Mr. Musial said, using his son's nickname.

"I don't want a scholarship," Stan said slowly, but firmly. "I want to try to sign with a baseball team."

"But you're just a boy," the father protested. "And how

much will they pay you for this signing?"

"About sixty-five dollars a month."

That really started the argument. The money wasn't much, and Mr. Musial couldn't see how Stan could ever hope to earn more. He said he wouldn't give his consent. It was then that Stan's mother spoke up. She reminded her husband that he came to America because it was a free country, and that a boy like Stan should have his own choice about his future.

The next year, 1938, young Stan had tryouts with Cleveland, New York, and Pittsburgh. Though he had signed an agreement with the Cardinals the year before, he thought they had forgotten him. They hadn't. He was finally signed and sent to Williamson, West Virginia, in the Mountain States League for the 1938 and '39 seasons.

The first year Stan reported late because he was still in high school. The next year he was out of school and married. He had met blonde-haired Lillian Labash at a local ball game, fallen in love with her, and married her. She always remained his faithful companion, fan, and devoted wife.

Stan won six and lost six, his first year, and was 9–2 in his second season before moving on to Daytona and that fateful meeting with a line drive. The next season (1941) he was at Springfield as an outfielder. The team's manager, Clay Hopper, didn't believe Stan couldn't pitch any more and insisted he try. He was bombed out fast.

Then Hopper didn't believe Stan could hit. But he finally gave him a try and Stan went on to hit .379 in just eighty-seven games, belting twenty-six homers and driving in ninety-four runs. Before the year ended he was sent to Rochester of the International League. He proved he could hit there, too, with a .326 average in fifty-four games. Then, at the tail end of that 1941 season, the Cards called him up for a look.

Playing in only twelve games, Stan whacked out twenty hits in forty-seven at-bats for a .426 mark. It was beginning to look as if the six foot, 180-pound youngster could hit anything. He'd be up with the Cards for a real shot the next season.

It was quite a season, that year of 1941. Stan started it in Springfield, trying to pitch with a dead arm, and he finished in St. Louis, hitting over .400 in twelve games, and getting a contract worth $4,250 for the next season.

When Stan reported to the Cards for the 1942 season, he was coming to one of the league's exciting, young teams. The Redbirds had finished second the year before; now everyone conceded that they had a fine chance to go all the way. With stars like Johnny Mize, Marty Marion, Enos Slaughter, Walker Cooper, Terry Moore, Mort Cooper, and Johnny Beazley, the team was strong in all departments.

Stan broke in slowly, being platooned early in the season. But by August, when the Cards started a real run at first place, he was in the lineup, playing right or left, every day. He had a big role in the St. Louis pennant push, which netted the Cards another N.L. flag. The team finished with a sensational 106–48 record, winning 43 of its last 52 games.

As for Stan, he hit a solid .315 in his rookie year. He had come to bat 467 times, slammed 10 homers, and banged home 72 runs. He also had thirty-two doubles and his first grand slammer off Rip Sewell of Pittsburgh.

Stan had a disappointing series, getting four hits in eighteen at-bats, but the Cards topped the Yanks in five games. The 21-year-old rookie was already on a world championship team. He headed home to Donora that October with $6,192 in his pocket (the World Series money) and tears in his eyes. He was a very happy man.

If Stan didn't play a major role in the Cards' 1942 success, it would be the last time anyone could make that claim. In his sophomore season, he paid no heed to the superstition that calls for a second-year man to slump. Instead, he set the league ablaze with his hot bat. He won his first batting title with a .357 average, had 220 hits in 617 at-bats, and was given the league's Most Valuable Player award. Though not very massive or strong looking, Stan played in every game and was to prove a durable ballplayer throughout the remainder of his career.

The Cards won another pennant in 1943, but this time lost the Series to the Yanks in five games, with Stan again failing to produce more than five singles.

But there was another pennant the next year, 1944, with Stan, a .347 hitter, driving home ninety-four runs. This time it wasn't the Yanks, but the crosstown St. Louis Browns facing the Cards. In a series that had the whole town turned on, the Cards won in six games. Stan had seven hits in this one, batting .304. He also got his first series homer.

By 1945, the war was raging and, like so many of the star players, Stan went to serve his country. He spent a year as a ship's repairman, playing as much ball as he could. Then he got his discharge. He was luckier than some of the others. Stars like DiMaggio, Williams, and Bob Feller lost about three peak years from their careers due to World War II. Stan missed a single season. And it didn't hurt his play one bit.

When he returned, his stance was even more exaggerated, the bend of the knee, the leaning forward, and the demonstrative wiggle of the hips. Stan once compared himself to a cat ready to strike.

"When a big cat stalks his prey," he said, "his tail always

swishes very slowly until just before he strikes. It helps keep him relaxed. I guess that's why I move my tail, too. Got to stay just relaxed enough until the pitcher throws."

Whatever he did, it worked. Stan hit .365 that year, won another bat title, slammed out 228 hits, and drove home 103 runs. He earned his second Most Valuable Player award and led his team to another World Series. This time, the Cards whipped the Boston Red Sox in seven games, with Stan contributing four key RBI's.

There wasn't much to complain about. In his first four full seasons in the majors, Stan's Cardinals won four pennants and three World Series. Stan the Man was not yet 26-years-old, and he was already a two-time MVP winner and recognized superstar in the National League. It's ironic, but the Cards didn't get into another World Series until 1964, one year after Musial hung up his spikes. But as of 1946, it didn't seem as if there were many more worlds to conquer.

Two years later, in 1948, Stan had his greatest all-around season at the plate. He had career highs of 39 home runs, 131 RBI's, 230 base hits, and a .376 batting average. He led the league in runs scored, hits, doubles, triples, RBI's, and in his batting average. He just missed in the home-run category by one, and that would have amounted to pretty much of a clean sweep.

As it was, Stan walked off with his third Most Valuable Player prize. And, yet, with all the fame and glory that was coming his way, he still had the humility to tell a writer:

"My biggest thrill in baseball is just putting on that uniform and playing every day. It's especially great right before the start of a new season."

And that's how Stan was different from so many other super ballplayers. Though he treasured his individual achievements, and looked upon his accomplishments with great pride, he was happy just to be playing. He didn't need the stardom. Not that he regretted being a superstar, but it was the game itself that held the joy and fascination for him. Everything else was a by-product.

The years following were amazingly consistent. His batting averages were .338, .346, .355, .336, .337, .330, .319, .310, .351, and .337. He was almost always over the one hundred RBI mark and hit between twenty-five and thirty-five home runs. Plus he got a lot of hits.

A statistical analysis of Musial's career bears out his remarkable consistency. He was a .300 hitter at every park he played at except Milwaukee. He batted .336 at home, .326 on the road. As an outfielder, he hit .336; as an infielder .324. He did some of his best hitting late in the season, in August and September, when lesser ballplayers wilted.

And he played where he could best help the team, never complaining about anything. His arm never fully regained its strength, but he ran well, and he covered first base as well as anyone. He never accepted the privileges that often go with superstar status. He always traveled with the team, for instance, even when he had trouble sleeping on trains and the club offered to fly him to certain cities.

When he received gifts or favors, he always shared them with those around him. He had a kind of crooked smile and slightly sloped eyes, under his neatly-trimmed dark hair. He looked happy and always had time for a teammate or friend.

"Stan Musial is probably the only superstar who never had a real enemy," said one long-time observer of the game. "Cobb, Ruth, Williams . . . all of them had someone who disliked them. Stan sure killed a lot of teams and a lot of pitchers with his bat, but no one ever held it against him as a person. You just couldn't."

There were plenty of milestones. On May 2, 1954, Stan the Man belted five home runs in a doubleheader against the Giants, three in the first game and another pair in the second. It tied a major league record. He also belted six home runs in all-star game competition, including a twelfth-inning shot that ended the 1955 game at Milwaukee.

Before the 1958 season, Stan the Man reached another milestone, a $100,000 contract from Card owner Gussie Busch. He celebrated twenty-two games into the season by collecting the 3,000th hit of his career. And he wasn't through yet.

Stan hit .337 that year, though his homer and RBI totals dipped sharply. He was almost thirty-eight years old. People were wondering when the slip would start.

During the off-season, Stan decided to rest a little more.

"I won't play too many exhibitions," he said, "won't run as much, and will try to take it a bit easier during the season."

The theory didn't work. Stan realized too late that he needed the action, not rest. He never got into good shape and had his first sub-par .300 season in eighteen years, hitting just .255 with only forty-four RBI's. There was some talk about his retiring. Stan listened, then said politely:

"I don't think I'm quite ready for that yet."

But his new manager, Solly Hemus, didn't agree. He wanted to go with young players, and had Stan in and out of the lineup early in 1960. But by June, no one else had worked out well in left. Stan had been keeping himself in shape, biding his time. When he got the chance he went on a 20–41 tear and proved he could still hit. He ending up at .275 that year with sixty-three RBI's, and in 1961 batted .288 with seventy ribbys.

At the end of that year, another new manager, Johnny Keane, took the 41-year-old Musial aside.

"Stan," he said quietly. "I'm convinced you could have played more these last few years. I think you can have a big year next season and I want you in there as much as possible. Get yourself in good shape this spring."

The Man took heed. He came back in 1962, at age forty-two, raring to go. Jumping out of the gate like a raw rookie, Stan hit from beginning to end. He had one slump, a 1–25 skein, but when he came out of it with a base hit off the Dodgers' Ron Perranoski, he passed the great Honus Wagner in total base hits for a National Leaguer.

Stan even made a run at an eighth batting title that year. He finished at .330, a throwback to years gone by, playing in 135 games and getting 143 hits, 19 home runs, and 82 RBI's. It was truly a remarkable season.

He tried it one more time, in 1963. This time it wasn't so easy. He passed Tris Speaker to go into second place on the all-time hit list, but there was little else. At forty-three, it was just too much, even for Stan the Man. He batted just .255, with twelve homers and fifty-eight RBI's. There was some excitement that year, when the Cards won nineteen of their final twenty games to tie the Dodgers for the flag. But the L.A. team won three straight in the playoffs, despite a dramatic Musial homer which temporarily delayed the inevitable. How he would have loved to have been in one more world series! He was a fighter right to the end.

On September 29, 1963, Stan Musial played his final regular season ball game. He banged out two singles, and drove home one final run in his last at-bat.

Retirement has been as sweet as his career. Stan is a highly respected citizen of St. Louis and the entire country. He is a

Cardinal vice-president, a millionaire, and has served in such prestigious positions as National Director of Physical Fitness.

Wherever you go, people have only kind words about Stan the Man Musial. He's a class guy all the way.

MICKEY CHARLES MANTLE

The Switcher

[1931–   ]

IT WAS A LAZY summer afternoon at Yankee Stadium in 1956. The Bronx Bombers, en route to another pennant, were playing the lowly Washington Senators in a game that meant virtually nothing. Righthander Pedro Ramos was on the mound for the Senators, as the Yanks' young slugger, Mickey Mantle, stepped in to hit.

A switch hitter, Mickey was digging in from the left side. Ramos tried to slip a fast one past him and Mickey let out with that big swing of his. The ball shot off the bat, heading high and deep to rightfield. The Washington rightfielder didn't move. He just watched the long drive sail far over his head. Everyone was looking up, even the fans in the upper deck.

The ball carried higher and higher. Then it hit, about two feet below the top of the stadium façade. Mickey Mantle had just missed becoming the first man to hit a fair ball out of Yankee Stadium. It had been a tremendous clout. Mickey circled the bases with a big grin on his face. He enjoyed hitting those long home runs, and he sure tagged plenty of them during his career.

Mickey was to hit that top façade again, in 1963. Some say

that second ball was hit even harder, and one scientist esti-
mated that it would have traveled some 620 feet if it had gone
on unimpeded. But these mammoth shots were nothing new
for Mickey. He had looked like a slugger from the first.

He stood an even six feet tall, and weighed two hundred
pounds. He was one of those ballplayers best described as
having muscles on top of his muscles. When Mickey Mantle
came to the plate, batting either right-handed or left-handed,
the rippling muscles along his forearms spelled power.

And he had power. Not only did the famed Yankee switch
hitter belt 536 home runs during his eighteen-year career, but
he hit some of the longest, highest, most majestic shots since
the heyday of Babe Ruth.

Yet this powerful man, with the picturesque power swing,
was plagued by injuries, major and minor, throughout his career. He often played with both legs taped from thigh to
ankle, and played well.

When he first joined the Yanks, he ran from home to first
as fast as any ballplayer in the league, maybe faster. He could
throw and field, and hit with awesome power. Years later,
before his retirement, injuries reduced him to a shell of his
former self. His legs were scarred from surgery and battered
from muscle pulls and tears. He could no longer throw due
to a painful shoulder injury. He still had the pure swing, but
young pitchers were striking him out because they knew he
lacked movement and agility at the plate.

Through it all, Mickey Mantle never complained, never
made excuses. He accepted his lot in life, and tried to cope
with it as best he could. It wasn't easy, hearing people say
that he might have been the greatest ever if not hobbled by
injuries. Might-have-beens don't count. You've got to live
with what you have, and Mickey Mantle knew it.

In the strange and changing world of the sports fan, Mickey was first a villain, then a hero. He came to the Yankees in 1951, the same year that the great Joe DiMaggio called it a career. When Mantle was mentioned as the new DiMaggio, some of Joltin' Joe's rooters were resentful. There could never be another Joe, they said.

The situation grew worse during the Korean War. Many ballplayers were being drafted during the 1952 and 1953 seasons. Mickey was called for a physical. He was rejected. Bad legs, the Army said. Many fans looked at the muscular Mantle and couldn't believe it.

When he was rejected in subsequent examinations, the hecklers began getting on him. Hadn't Willie Mays, the Giants' young superstar, been taken? Then, why not Mantle? He was called a slacker, a draft-dodger, and a coward in every city around the league. Mickey was an innocent victim of circumstance, but the constant taunts were hard for him to take.

The truth was that Mickey was indeed unfit for service, just as he was so often unfit for baseball. As a high-school football player, he had been kicked in the leg and developed osteomyelitis, a disease of the bone marrow, one that can recur. Furthermore, he had suffered a severe knee injury in the 1951 World Series and had undergone surgery during the off-season. So as early as 1952, his legs were permanently damaged and would never be the same again.

Throughout the 1950's, Mickey was greeted with a mixture of cheers and jeers, even in his own Yankee Stadium. Then came 1961, when Mickey and teammate Roger Maris both began chasing Babe Ruth's record of sixty home runs in a season.

When it appeared that both sluggers would have a chance

at the record, the sentiment swung to Mantle. After all, he was steeped in Yankee tradition, the big slugging superstar who spearheaded the latest Bomber dynasty.

Maris? He was an outsider, brought in from Kansas City, and considered somewhat of a flash in the pan. When stories of Roger's surliness and problems with the press began creeping into the papers, the fans really began rooting for the Mick. And when Maris cracked the record with sixty-one homers, Mickey was the guy they felt sorry for, even though he had hit a personal high of fifty-four homers himself.

Nineteen hundred and sixty-one signaled the start of a growing popularity that was to continue right to the end. In his last years, Mantle was the idol of baseball, receiving standing ovations at almost every park he visited. Everyone knew about Mickey's courage, how he played with pain, how his great talent was eroded by injuries. The reaction was a mixture of sympathy and admiration.

Though Mickey's accomplishments in the big leagues are great, most experts agree that he would have achieved an even greater record if he hadn't lost so much time to injuries. For instance, Mickey was hobbled much of his final four years, and his batting average fell sharply. He hit just .255, .245, and .237 in three of those seasons. It caused his lifetime mark to drop below .300 (to .298), and this bothered him greatly.

Still, there are many plusses. He belted 536 homers among his 2,415 base hits. He won the American League triple crown in 1956 with a .353 average, fifty-two home runs, and 130 runs batted in. The following year, he batted .365, but lost the hitting title to Ted Williams.

Three times, in 1956, 1957, and 1962, he was the American League's Most Valuable Player. He holds the record for

World Series homers with eighteen, and set Series marks for runs batted in, runs scored, total bases, long hits, walks, and strikeouts.

He also has the dubious achievement of striking out more than any other man in history. He fanned 1,710 times. But in setting that mark, he passed another pretty fair ballplayer, Babe Ruth. And it has been said that Ruth and Mantle were the two most consistent long home run hitters in the game, slamming the highest, longest drives over a period of time.

Mickey Charles Mantle was born on October 20, 1931, at Spavinaw, Oklahoma. Soon after he was born, his family moved to Commerce, the place he always considered his home town.

His father, Elven "Mutt" Mantle, was a tough miner who loved baseball. He named his first son after his favorite ballplayer, Mickey Cochran. The Mickey is a given name, not a nickname for Michael. It was the elder Mantle who encouraged his son to play ball. Mickey admired and respected his father, and at first played the game to please him.

"No boy ever loved his father more than I did," Mickey would say. "He was a strong, vigorous man, who loved life and loved his family."

He also loved baseball, and he practiced with Mickey diligently, teaching him to hit and field, and starting him off as a switch hitter at an early age. Mickey himself admits that his father pushed him, perhaps more than he should have. But, fortunately, the youngster never resented it.

"It's really a wonder that I didn't turn against baseball," he often said. "Because when you get right down to it, I really had it forced on me when I was young. But instead of hating it, I loved it, and I never had to be asked twice if I wanted to practice or play. And that's the way I've always felt about the game. It's meant everything to me."

Mickey played the infield as a youngster. He says it's because they played on a flat, hard field, and any ball that got past the outfielders would roll and roll and roll. He didn't feel like chasing it that far.

None of that mattered when Mickey was hitting. He quickly became the best hitter in his age group, whether it was in the Pee Wee League, the Gabby Street League, or the Commerce-Picher team, in all of which he starred during his formative years in Commerce.

Pretty soon he was earning a reputation as a budding young slugger. As a teen-ager, he once clouted three long homers in a game, the last one going into a river behind centerfield, some five hundred feet away. The fans went wild. They passed around a hat, collected $54.00, and gave it to the youngster. Mickey was overjoyed. But several days later he learned he'd have to return the money if he wanted to retain his amateur standing in high school. He lost the money, but not the thrill of his first taste of play-for-pay.

When he was seventeen, Mickey was playing with the Baxter Springs team in the Ban Johnson League, which was for high-school-age boys. The team was at Parsons, Kansas, when Yankee scout Tom Greenwade looked twice at the husky shortstop.

Sure enough, it was the same youngster Greenwade had seen the year before, when he had received a tip about Mickey. What he saw the first time was a skinny kid. Now he was looking at a powerful young man who could hit. He was amazed at the way Mickey had filled out.

Greenwade quickly sought out Mutt Mantle.

"Listen, Mr. Mantle," he said. "The Yankees are definitely

interested in your boy. Please don't sign with anyone before I get back here on Sunday."

Then the scout left to report to his bosses. Mutt Mantle smiled. He knew his son was close to receiving a big league offer. It was something both father and son had always wanted.

When Greenwade returned, he offered Mickey a $140-per-month contract to play with a Class D team in the Yankee organization.

"Are you kidding?" Mutt Mantle said. "Mickey can make that much playing Sunday ball around Spavinaw and working during the week."

The two men continued to bargain, and when Greenwade threw in a $1,150 bonus, the deal was closed.

One year later, in 1950, Mickey was at Joplin, Missouri, where he batted .383 in 137 games. He banged out 26 homers among his 199 hits, and drove in 136 runs. The only problem was his 55 errors in the infield. He just didn't look like much of an infielder.

That was when the Yankees decided to make the youngster an outfielder. DiMaggio was nearing the end of the line and they were starting to look around their organization for a replacement.

In 1951, Mickey was called up to the big club. He started slowly, and was sent down to Kansas City of the American Association for more seasoning. After a few weeks of battering minor league pitching, Mickey was recalled to stay. Playing rightfield alongside DiMag, Mickey hit .267, with thirteen home runs and sixty-five RBI's, and the Yankees won the pennant. The Mick had come to bat just 341 times, making his rookie slugging stats even more impressive.

But the injury jinx started to stalk him in the World Series that year when, trotting over to back up DiMaggio, he caught his foot in a drainage ditch and his knee buckled. The result was his first operation.

Off the field, there were also high and low points. Early in the spring of 1951, Mickey had married his Oklahoma sweetheart, Merlyn Louise Johnson. There he was, newly married and a rookie with the New York Yankees. Things couldn't have been better.

But shortly after his baseball low point, the knee operation, his beloved father died from Hodgkins disease, a form of cancer, at age forty. Mickey grieved over his father's passing, and became more determined than ever to make it big. He'll always regret that proud Mutt Mantle never saw him attain superstardom.

In 1952, with DiMaggio retired, Mickey moved to centerfield. He had some pretty big shoes to fill, but he never let the tremendous pressure overcome him. The next four seasons (1952–55), he hit .311, .295, .300, and .306. He was also averaging twenty-seven homers and ninety-five RBI's per season, but he still hadn't come up with the big year everyone was waiting for.

Then came the 1956 season, and the Mick finally put it all together. Hitting from both sides of the plate with authority, he won the triple crown, leading the league in hitting (.353), homers (52), and runs batted in (130). He was also the American League's Most Valuable Player, and he clouted three more homers in the Series against the Dodgers.

To top off his greatest season up to that time, he showed his prowess as a fielder with a running backhand catch of a Gil Hodges drive to save Don Larsen's perfect game in the Series.

As a hitter, Mickey was not a carbon-copy from the right

and left sides of the plate. He had the same slightly closed stance, bat held high and still. But he had a more level cut from the right and didn't hit as many long drives. Baseball people always said he was a better hitter from the right, and his batting average was constantly higher from the starboard side. Later in his career, there was some pressure on him to bat strictly right-handed, but he refused, remaining a switcher to the end.

Furthermore, batting, in Yankee Stadium he had a much better chance for homers when he hit left-handed. The Stadium has a shallow rightfield and a deep leftfield, and right-handed batters have always had a tough time hitting the long ball unless they pull it right down the line.

In 1957, Mickey had another fine year. His batting average was up to .365, but his homer and RBI totals fell off slightly, to thirty-four and ninety-four. Still, it was good enough for him to win his second straight MVP Award.

On the field, Mickey continued to perform well. But he was beginning to show the wear and tear of his many injuries. He wasn't running the bases with as much daring as before, and he had trouble making quick cuts, sudden starts and stops.

Pretty soon, his injury list read like a major medical logbook. He had a cyst removed from his knee in 1954, a pulled groin muscle in '55, a left knee sprain in '56, a shoulder injury in '57, a broken finger in '59. Even in the big year of 1961, when Mickey battled Maris for the home run record, he was slowed in the final weeks of the season by a hip abscess.

Yet the 1961 season was a personal triumph for Mickey. He gained his greatest popularity up to that time with the fans, and many of the experts were beginning to appreciate his true value as a ballplayer.

"Maybe Maris broke the record," said one writer. "But don't forget, he was batting ahead of Mickey. So he got the good pitches. Without Mickey behind him, he'd have never broken the record."

There was no taking away from Maris' season. Roger had 140 RBI's to go along with his 61 homers, but his batting average was a mediocre .269. By contrast, Mickey knocked in 128 runs and had a .317 batting mark. It was a truly superior season for him.

The next year Mickey moved back into the spotlight with his third Most Valuable Player Award. He had a .321 batting average in that 1962 season, though he hit just thirty homers and drove in eighty-nine runs. He had his last big year in 1964, the season the Yankees won their final pennant before the collapse. Mick batted .303 that year, with 35 homers and 111 RBI's.

It was a big year for him in more ways than one. He had broken a foot in Baltimore the year before (1963) and played just sixty-five games. Now, at the age of thirty-three, he proved to himself that he could still play.

But it really wasn't like the old days. During the season his shoulder began hurting. In the 1964 World Series, Cardinal runners challenged his arm, which lacked the power it had had several years before. He atoned with eight hits and three more Series homers, giving him the record of eighteen. Still, it was the beginning of the end.

The next year he underwent shoulder surgery and his average slipped to .255. He also had elbow and knee injuries. His physical condition was worsening, and sympathetic teammates winced as they saw Mickey being taped, thigh to ankle, before every game. It was hard to believe. The Mick still had the beautiful physique—the bull neck, massive

shoulders and arms, and well-proportioned legs. Many observers figured he was just brittle, but Doctor Sidney Gay-
nor, the Yanks' team physician, said no.

"Mickey just made too many demands on his body," the
doctor said. "He was unfortunate to get injured early in his
career, and the starting, stopping, and pivoting just continued
to aggravate the problem. Mickey didn't know how to go at
less than full speed."

Some thought he should have quit after the 1964 season.
But he didn't. He declined rapidly after that, and so did the
Yankees. The Bombers were no longer a powerhouse, and
Mantle, the symbol of that power, just couldn't find the old
skills any more.

Amazingly, Mickey came to bat 440 and 435 times his final
two seasons. This was better than three of the four injury-
plagued years before that. He was playing first base now,
trying to save his legs. But he was striking out more and hitting below .250. He averaged twenty homers and fifty-four
runs batted in during 1967 and 1968, well below his former
standards.

Mickey reported to spring training in 1969, worked out a
few times, then made the announcement everyone had been
waiting for.

"I was going to give it a try this year," he said, "but I just
don't think I can make it. I've had several bad years in a row
now, and my lifetime average is below .300. That's been one
of my greatest disappointments. I was actually dreading this
coming season.

"I can't do the things I used to do out there and this hurts,
too. It's no good for me, the other Yankees, and the fans.
It's becoming increasingly embarrassing to have young kids
throwing the ball past me. So it's over . . . and I'm glad."

Painfully honest, the words were hard for Mickey to say. No player likes to admit that his skills are gone. But Mickey was thirty-seven, and he knew the time had come.

What to do in retirement? Mickey now spends more time with his wife and four sons. Several business ventures have gone sour, but he put in a successful stint as a broadcaster for NBC. He plays a lot of golf and enjoys "playing" in old-timers' games.

Perhaps there'll be a return to the diamond some day. Mickey has talked about managing, and even coached for a month with the Yankees to see how he liked a non-playing field role. The game his father taught him so many years before still seems to have a magic hold on him.

On June 8, 1969, the Yankees held an appreciation day for Mickey. They announced that his number "7" would be retired, as were the "3," "4," and "5" of the Babe, Lou, and DiMag.

Mickey was traveling in fast company with those three greats, all right. But there was little doubt in anyone's mind that the slugging switcher belonged.

WILLIE HOWARD MAYS
The Say Hey Kid

[1931–   ]

In the whole, long history of baseball, no one has loved playing the sport more than Willie Mays. It doesn't matter whether it's a world series, an exhibition game, an all-star encounter, or just a game of stickball with some kids on St. Nicholas Place—when Willie Mays is playing ball, he's happy.

He came into the majors with a childlike exuberance that made him an immediate national favorite. His play over the years continued to reflect that quality. To Willie, baseball would always be a fun game.

His career began with the Giants in New York, before he moved with that team to San Francisco. Then, at the age of forty-one and in the twilight of his playing days, he was traded to the New York Mets, returning to the city he had always loved. And the whole town turned out to welcome him home.

Willie Mays, every bit as talented as he is enthusiastic, can do it all on a baseball diamond. He can run, field, hit, and throw. And if he's not the top ballplayer of his time, he's certainly the most exciting—Mays, running out from under his cap while chasing a long fly; Mays, stealing second in a cloud of dust; Mays, making a basket catch with the best pair of hands since DiMaggio; Mays, clouting a long home run to win a ball game; Mays, leaping high to make another outstanding catch and throwing the runner out at home. Mays! Mays! Mays!

That's his game, speed and excitement. A power bat, rocket arm, and flashing feet. Sound like Superman? Well, almost.

He's a .300 lifetime hitter, has more than 650 home runs, and has topped 3,000 hits. There isn't a baseball fan alive today who hasn't been thrilled to disbelief by one of Willie's wonderful plays on the diamond.

Perhaps the most famous one occurred in the first game of the 1954 World Series. The then New York Giants were playing the Cleveland Indians at the old Polo Grounds in New York. It was a 2–2 game in the top of the eighth. The Indians had runners on first and second with Vic Wertz at the plate.

Wertz was a left-handed batter and he tied into the first pitch from lefty Don Liddle, sending a tremendous drive to deep centerfield. The split-second the ball was hit, Willie turned his back on home plate and started running. Once or twice he glanced over his shoulder, but he didn't break stride. Would he make it? There was some 485 feet of ground to cover at the Polo Grounds, and it looked as if Willie would run over every inch of it.

Still digging at full tilt, Willie reached up, the ball dropped over his shoulder and into his glove, some 460 feet from home plate. Without hesitating, he whirled and threw toward first, the ball coming to the bag on two hops, almost doubling up the runner. It was one of the greatest catches and throws of all time.

Everyone has a Mays story or two. Mets General Manager Bob Scheffing tells one about Willie misjudging a fly during his rookie season of 1951.

"The ball fell past his glove," Scheffing said, "but he suddenly reached out and caught the ball in his bare hand."

It took only a year or two for the legend to grow. The "Say Hey" kid was a superstar his second season in the bigs, and his performance never slipped below its original quality. Willie always gave more than 100 per cent on the field—so much more, in fact, that in later years he'd often suffered from exhaustion near the end of the season. But he knew only one way to play the game. His own philosophy was simple.

"Play ball in the way that it's most natural for you," he said. "But get out and play every day. You got to work at it day in and day out if you ever want to be good."

Willie worked at being a ballplayer ever since he can remember. He was born on May 6, 1931, in Westfield, Alabama. His father, Willie Howard Mays, Sr., had spent some time with the Birmingham Black Barons in the Negro Leagues before retiring to work in the steel mills. He taught his young son the fundamentals of the game early, and young Willie was hooked. Nothing but baseball mattered to him.

The elder Mays always had time for his energetic little boy. And when he had to go to the mills, Willie would seek out companions his own age. Whenever his mother asked him where he was going, Willie had the same answer.

"Play ball," was all he said.

And he played and played. Before long it was obvious that he had more than average talent. There was never any doubt about what he wanted to do. Willie wasn't much for school. He just passed his time in the Westfield school system, dreaming of the day when he could play baseball full time.

When he was sixteen, he already had the skills that labeled him a future star. That was in 1947, the same year that Jackie Robinson came to the major leagues. Now Willie would have a chance to play there, too. Otherwise, he would have been one of the best ballplayers the Negro Leagues ever had. Willie Mays was born to play baseball, no matter where, or how, or with whom.

By the time he was nineteen, the Giants had offered him a contract and he jumped at the chance. He wasn't even interested in money, just in playing ball. He was a free-spirited youngster, naive in many ways, yet just a few years away from national recognition.

He spent the 1950 season at Trenton and batted .353 in eighty-one games. The Giants were getting excited. They kept hearing stories about the youngster with all the speed, enthusiasm, and talent. They soon assigned him to their top farm club at Minneapolis for the 1951 season. Now they'd really see what he could do.

It took just thirty-five games for him to show them. Willie came to the plate 149 times and pounded out 71 hits. That's an average of .477, and you can't do much better than that. Willie was on a hitting spree that made him seem almost super-human.

In New York, the Giants were licking their chops. The New Yorkers had a solid, veteran team, with good pitching and good hitting. But they were missing the final link, the spark that could make them a serious contender. Fiery Leo Durocher, the manager, knew he had to make a move. First he considered a trade to strengthen the team. But nothing materialized. Finally, he made his decision.

"Get Mays up here," he said.

So up came Willie to the big city, bringing with him six bats, a shaving kit, a toothbrush, and a big, happy grin.

The Giants watched him in practice. He looked every bit as good as his press clippings had claimed. Just 5' 11" and 180 pounds, Willie was rope-muscle hard. At the plate, he whistled liners all over the field, and, in the vast area that was the Polo Grounds outfield, he roamed like a wild colt, grabbing everything in sight with his special basket catch, squeezing the ball at his waist, instead of over his head like most outfielders. And his throwing arm was as strong as they come.

When owner Horace Stoneham asked Durocher how he liked his young outfielder, Leo answered:

"I'll marry him."

He almost did. From the day Willie joined the Giants, he came under the personal care and guidance of Leo Durocher. Leo had a reputation as a hard-boiled, driving leader, with a short fuse and explosive temper. If a player did something wrong, he let him know about it. But never once did he so much as raise his voice to Willie. The youngster was like an adopted son to him. Also, there was little Willie did on the diamond that was wrong.

The Giants went on a road trip as soon as Willie joined the team, and the strange ballparks must have made him nervous. He didn't get a hit in five trips during his first game at Philadelphia, and was zero for twelve before the Series ended.

Willie was upset. He had never been so discouraged about his hitting before. He approached Durocher and told the manager he wasn't ready.

"I think you better send me back to Minneapolis," he said.

Leo stood up and put his arm around the youngster.

"Don't you worry about a thing," he told him. "If you don't get a hit in fifty times up, you're still my centerfielder.

Don't ever forget that."

The next night Willie stepped up against the Braves' great lefty, Warren Spahn, and got his first big league hit, a long home run over the leftfield wall. He wasn't out of the woods yet. He failed to hit in fourteen more trips, but Leo and outfielder Monte Irvin kept after him, encouraging him and urging him to relax.

Finally, he started finding the groove, the base hits began to fall in, and the Giants began to make a move. It was the year of the Miracle of Coogan's Bluff. Trailing the Dodgers by thirteen games in August, the New Yorkers staged a remarkable comeback and tied it up on the last day of the season. The ensuing playoff had the city of New York in an uproar, and the finish will be remembered as long as there is a game of baseball.

Trailing the Dodgers by two runs in the final inning of the deciding game, the Giants put a pair of runners on base with one out. Third baseman Bobby Thomson was up, facing righthander Ralph Branca, and young Willie Mays was on deck.

Willie never got to hit. Thomson belted Branca's fastball into the leftfield seats, the "shot heard round the world," and the Giants won the pennant in the most dramatic ending in baseball history.

As the Giants got ready to face the Yanks in the Series, Durocher told a reporter that "the kid had a lot to do with winning the pennant."

"The Kid" was Willie Mays. Playing in 121 games that year, Willie overcame the early slump to bat .274. He hit twenty home runs and had sixty-eight RBI's. There was little doubt that he was a coming star.

Although the Giants lost the Series that year, no one

seemed to care much. The pennant finish had been so great that the Series turned out to be anticlimactic.

Willie started the next season with all the optimism in the world. Then came the news. The Korean War was in full swing and he was being drafted. There was nothing he could do but go. Many fans were resentful that Willie had to go while crosstown rival Mickey Mantle was deferred. Mickey bore the brunt of their wrath, but he had a genuine leg ailment that made him unfit for service.

With Mays gone, the Giants failed to repeat in 1952 and 1953, but when he returned in '54, they put it all together again. Willie was superb. He showed no signs of having been away. He led the league in hitting with a .345 mark, belted 41 home runs, and drove in 110 runs. For his efforts, he was named the Most Valuable Player in the National League.

In the World Series sweep of the Indians, it was Willie's fabulous catch of Vic Wertz's drive that broke the back of the Cleveland attack. If he hadn't caught that ball, the entire Series might have turned around.

Willie's life off the field was quiet in those days. He had an apartment in Harlem, near the Polo Grounds, and spent much of his spare time playing stickball on the streets with the neighborhood kids. He could play ball twenty-four hours a day and be happy.

He had a friendly word for everyone, but he couldn't remember names. So his standard greeting was "Say, hey," whenever he addressed anyone. From that came his nickname, the "Say Hey Kid."

It fit Willie well. He was like a kid on the field, running, hitting, and catching everything around him. When he belted fifty-one homers in 1955, it was obvious that he had also matured into a genuine slugger.

Although the Giants failed to finish on top again from 1955 to 1957, Willie put together three good years. Then, with attendance dwindling to nothing, the Giants announced that they would follow the Dodgers to the West Coast for the 1958 season. The New York Giants were about to become the San Francisco Giants.

Willie wasn't happy about leaving New York. "I've always played here, I love the Polo Grounds, and love the people," he said. "My heart will always be in New York."

Maybe it was a foreshadowing. When the Giants opened in San Francisco, the fans were reluctant to accept Willie as one of their own. He had a great year in '58, batting .347, with twenty-nine homers and ninety-seven RBI's. He also stole thirty-one bases. But the fans were surprisingly cold. They adopted a big Puerto Rican rookie, Orlando Cepeda, as their hero. Maybe they figured Cepeda didn't have roots in New York. Willie, they thought, would never truly be theirs.

Durocher was no longer around, either. The Giants were to have several managers in the next years. Only one, Herman Franks, who was to become Willie's friend and financial advisor, ever came close to having the rapport that Leo had with the slugger. Those early years in New York may have been Willie's happiest ever.

But he had some great years on the Coast. He continued to belt home runs and had a .300-plus batting average for the next five seasons.

By then, Willie was already making his mark in the annual all-star game, the mid-summer classic that features the top ballplayers in each league. Every summer, no matter where the game was held, Willie Mays was the star. He ran wild, exhibiting all his great skills to the entire country. Managers would usually bat him first, so he could get on base and do his stuff. He holds most of the all-star game hitting records, and hasn't missed one since 1954.

Perhaps his most gratifying year on the Coast was 1962. Not only did Willie belt 49 homers and drive in 141 runs, but the Giants won another pennant. And Willie Mays got to go home, for the first time in eight seasons.

There was a new National League team in New York— the Mets—and they were playing in the Polo Grounds. More than fifty thousand fans jammed the old ballpark the first time the Giants came to town. When Willie was introduced, they went wild. For ten solid minutes they stood and cheered.

There were banners all over the place.

WELCOME HOME, WILLIE

NEW YORK LOVES THE METS, AND WILLIE MAYS

DON'T LEAVE US, WILLIE

It was a touching tribute. Willie shuffled nervously, tipped his cap, then doffed it and waved to his fans, none of whom had forgotten for a moment the great baseball he had played for them when the Giants were in New York.

As usual, Willie came through. Batting, as always, from the right side with a slightly open stance, he belted one high and deep into the leftfield seats. They cheered again. And when he made a couple of fine catches, running in that peculiar shuffling style of his, they cheered some more. It was Willie's night, all the way.

There was a strange sidelight to Willie's return to New York. The late Russ Hodges, who broadcast the Giants' games in New York and later in San Francisco, said that Willie's return to the Polo Grounds seemed to trigger a new era in fan appreciation on the West Coast.

"It's funny," Hodges said, "but the fans were slow to accept Willie in San Francisco. Cepeda was their man. But when they watched on television that night and saw Willie welcomed back to New York, they seemed to realize that he was theirs, after all. They had him, not New York. After that night, the cheers for him in San Francisco grew louder and longer with each passing year."

In some respects, the 1962 season was a last hurrah. The Giants lost the World Series to the Yanks in seven games. It would be their last pennant of the Mays era. Willie had some grand years after that, belting fifty-two homers and hitting .317 in 1965, for instance, but in the second half of the sixties, he began slowing down.

Maybe it was his pace, the all-out way in which he played the game. He stopped stealing bases, going from a high of forty to about five or six a year. But, otherwise, he still played every inning to the hilt.

His managers said he should be rested, especially in July, August, and September. They didn't want him playing double-headers, or day games that followed night contests. But it seemed as if the Giants were always in a pennant race and they needed Willie more than ever in the stretch run. He began to fade each August and September, and on several occasions became dizzy and faint from fatigue, necessitating a few days of complete rest. After 1965, he never hit .300 again.

But his great record over the years was adding up. The milestones began to come. He hit home run number 400, then number 500, and finally 600. There was some talk of his passing Ruth as he forged into second place on the all-time list. But his production dropped off after 1965. He hit just 22 in 1967, 23 the next year, and 13 the year after that. He had

somewhat of a comeback year in 1970, with 28 round trippers, 83 RBI's, and a .291 average, but at 39, the end was in
sight. Early in the 1972 season, Henry Aaron of the Braves
passed Willie in career home runs. Now Aaron was chasing
the Babe, Willie's race over.

There were some other unhappy moments. A bad marriage
caused him some difficulty, and several outside investments
foundered. While he was making more than $100,000 an-
nually, his financial future was in doubt. That's when Herman Franks stepped in and provided Willie with the sage advice that has given him financial stability.

By the end of 1970, Willie reached another goal when he
collected his 3,000th base hit. He and Aaron are the only two
ballplayers with 3,000 hits and 600 home runs. Willie is also
among the all-time leaders in games, at-bats, runs scored, and
runs batted in.

When the 1972 season opened, Willie's future was in serious doubt. The players' strike set his training schedule back
and he was in and out of the lineup when the season started.
At forty-one years of age, it was beginning to look as if he
could no longer do the job. Occasionally there was a flash of
brilliance in the field, where he hadn't really slowed up. But
his bat looked awfully heavy, and he couldn't seem to play
more than a few games in a row.

The Giants were also having troubles at the gate. There
was talk that they no longer wanted to carry Willie's big salary. The thought of trading him made sentimentalists cringe.
No one dreamed that Willie Mays would ever be anything
but a Giant. Willie himself was unhappy about sitting the
bench. And when the Giants wouldn't give him a guarantee
of a job when he finished playing, he became unnerved.

There was really only one place he could go, one place he

would go. That was back to New York. The rumors began spreading. There was a series of secret meetings, involving club officials and Willie himself. Then the news broke. The Giants had traded Mays to the New York Mets, whose owner, Joan Payson, had a sense of the romantic. She felt Willie should come home where he belonged.

When the terms of the deal were announced, they were obviously to Willie's liking. He would continue as a player as long as it was felt he could contribute to the team's success. But then he would be guaranteed a job within the organization for an undetermined period of time. It gave him the security he wanted, and returned him to the city he had always loved.

They welcomed him in droves. There was a parade, television interviews, countless press conferences, and a reception at city hall. Met fans in Shea Stadium (the Polo Grounds had long been demolished) had waited ten years for this to happen. As far as they were concerned, Willie never belonged in San Francisco. This was always his home.

Willie was batting just .184 with three RBI's when he joined the team. He played his first game on May 14, against, of all teams, the Giants. With the score tied at 4–4 late in the game, Willie came up.

"Now, Willie, now," one fan pleaded.

"Show 'em where you always belonged," another said.

"Pleeeeeese, pleeeeeeese, pleeeeeeese," a young woman squealed.

Willie dug in. The body was still lean and hard, but the face more deeply lined and not as cheerful as it had once been. Willie squinted and waited for the pitch. He got it and whipped the bat around. A rising line drive headed out toward leftfield. It kept climbing . . . it was going . . . out of the park! Mays had done it. He raced around the bases, a big grin on his face, and a packed house screaming in delight at a moment they'd never forget. It was Willie's first home run of the season, number 647 lifetime. It was one of the greatest moments of his career.

In the following weeks, Willie's bat won a few more games. He was still highly respected in the field, and when Manager Yogi Berra put him in the lineup, he went to centerfield, with the regular centerfielder, Tommie Agee, moving over to right or left. On some days he played first, and handled the job like a professional.

When Willie joined the team, the Mets were in a pennant race, and many thought he'd help recreate the Miracle of Coogan's Bluff, some twenty-one years earlier.

But the team ran into a series of crippling injuries. Willie was forced to play more than he wanted, and his legs began to trouble him. A nagging knee injury made the second half of the year painful. He finished the season with a .250 batting average, eight homers, and twenty-two runs batted in. The totals were almost embarrassing in light of his former production at the plate.

What awaits Willie now? Cooperstown? Obviously. And lasting admiration from a city to which he has given so much. In a way, it's sad that his entire career couldn't have been played in New York. But, then again, maybe it's not.

This way, both sides of the country had the supreme pleasure and enjoyment of watching Willie Mays play baseball. And no one who saw him will ever forget. Perhaps it was Mets' relief pitcher Tug McGraw who best summed up the Mays era in baseball.

"Willie Mays," said Tug, "is the essence of the athletic spirit."

HENRY LOUIS AARON

Hammerin' Hank

[1934–   ]

I DON'T WANT to be anything or anyone special. I just want to be remembered as plain Henry Aaron."

Words from a modest superstar. Only he won't get his wish. With all the records being set by Henry Aaron, he's going to be remembered as someone very special for a long time to come.

Still, his request to remain almost anonymous tells you much about Henry Aaron, the ballplayer, as well as Henry Aaron, the man. He has been called Hammerin' Hank, but he has also been referred to as the Quiet Superstar. That's because of the way he does things on the field.

Henry Aaron never makes a lot of noise. His cap doesn't go sailing in the breeze when he runs under a fly ball or legs out a double. He plays the game without gimmicks. He simply does everything superbly. Some say he does it better than any ballplayer of the modern era. A look at his record seems to bear this out.

At the end of the 1972 baseball season, Henry Aaron was close to the top of the all-time list in the following categories—games played, at-bats, runs, hits, total bases, runs batted in, extra base hits, and home runs.

Of all these, perhaps the last one is the most important. For Henry Aaron is pursuing one of baseball's greatest marks, Babe Ruth's career record of 714 home runs.

For years, the experts said this standard would never be topped. But slowly, surely, and with remarkable consistency, Henry Aaron has gained ground. At the close of the 1972 campaign, Hammerin' Hank had 673 round trippers, 41 to go. Barring injury, he's a good bet to top the mark in another two seasons. And if he continues to play close to his usual level of excellence, he could not only break Ruth's record but land at the top in some of the other areas, too. That's how consistently outstanding Henry Aaron has been over the years.

He has been with the Braves since 1954, playing with the team in both Milwaukee and Atlanta. He has been a batting champion, a home run king, a Most Valuable Player, a world series winner, and an all-star. His earnings of approximately $200,000 a year make him one of the highest-paid players of all time. In his quiet, unassuming way, Henry Aaron has done it all. He takes great pride in his performance, in his physical condition, and in his records.

Yet his idea of a good time is a simple night at home with his wife and four children. This soft-spoken, quiet man has resisted superstardom for years. Now he can no longer stay out of the limelight. In the next several years, the Henry Aaron story is going to be told and retold, until every sports fan in America knows all about the unassuming man with the explosive bat.

Henry Louis Aaron was born in Mobile, Alabama, on February 5, 1934. His parents, Herbert and Estella Aaron, came to Mobile two years before he was born. They had lived in the small farm town of Camden, working in the fields and barely making a living. Many black families in the area faced the same hardships.

Herbert Aaron was a hard-working man. After coming to Mobile, he got a job as a boilermaker's assistant. Henry was the third of seven children, so Mr. Aaron always had plenty of mouths to feed.

Young Henry was a loner from the first. He really didn't enjoy playing with the neighboring boys but preferred to stay at home, helping his mother and playing with his brothers.

Mrs. Aaron remembers his spending hours in their small backyard, spinning a top and then just watching it. He'd do it over and over again. Until one day: "I went out there to see what he was doing," Estella Aaron recalls. "And he was playing with the top, as usual. Only this time he was hitting it with a baseball bat."

His interest in baseball goes way back. As a young boy he'd often go out to Hartwell Field in Mobile and watch the barnstorming major league teams that passed through on their way north to begin the regular season. He'd sit for hours and watch stars like Joe DiMaggio and Stan Musial. The game had a profound effect on him even then. When he was only eight years old, he walked into the house and announced to his parents:

"When I grow up, I'm gonna play baseball as good as Joe DiMaggio."

The Aarons didn't take him seriously. But they did want him to get an education. And besides, in those days, blacks couldn't play baseball except in the Negro Leagues.

Henry was just entering his teens when World War II ended. Many of the top baseball stars had been in the service, and Henry missed seeing them for several years. Now he was back at Hartwell Field, watching his old favorites in action once more. Only this time, something was different. The Brooklyn Dodgers had a new player named Jackie Robinson. This rekindled dreams of playing in the big leagues for black youngsters everywhere. And Henry really started thinking about making baseball his career.

It wasn't long after that Henry became one of the best softball players in Mobile. There were so few hardball leagues around that most of the boys played softball. Henry could hit better than anyone else, and he did it cross-handed. Batting from the right side, he held his left hand above his right on the bat. This was the opposite of the way it should be done, but somehow, Henry got away with it.

He continued hitting that way at Central High School, where he led his team to the Negro High School Championship. And when he was just fifteen, a man named Ed Scott approached him during a playground game.

"How would you like to make a little money, Aaron?" he asked.

Henry was skeptical. He thought Ed Scott was some kind of con man. But then Scott added, "Playing baseball."

Ed Scott wanted Henry to play for the Mobile Black Bears, a semipro team with a fine reputation in the area. Henry had to convince his mother, but he finally got the OK. Before long, he was a star. Pay was usually three to five dollars a game, depending on how well a player did. Henry did so well that he often got ten dollars a game from the team's owner.

While he was still fifteen, Henry went for a tryout with the Brooklyn Dodgers, who were holding a tryout camp in Mobile. But the youngster wasn't very aggressive, and the older boys simply pushed him out of the way when he tried to hit or go out to shortstop, the position he favored at the time.

Henry was very disappointed, but he began playing even better for the Bears. Soon after that, the Indianapolis Clowns, one of the best Negro League teams in the country, came into town to play the Bears. Henry slammed a pair of singles and a double that day, and he looked great in the field. After the game, Bunny Downs, a road manager of the Clowns, approached him.

Downs gave Henry the third degree. "How old are you, kid? You still in high school? When do you get out?" Henry answered quietly and politely. Then Downs finally got to the point.

"OK, Aaron, I want you to play some baseball for the Clowns. How about it?"

Henry couldn't believe what he heard. He tried to act casual and said, "Sure, why not?"

"Good," replied Downs. "I'll send you a contract as soon as you graduate from high school."

The young ballplayer didn't want to get his hopes up. But shortly after Henry graduated from the Josephine Allen Institute (where his parents had sent him for his senior year), a contract from the Clowns arrived by mail. Once again, Henry had to convince his parents that he really wanted baseball. They still thought an education was important, but finally said he could play.

So, in May of 1952, Henry prepared to leave home for the first time, and he was heading for the training camp of the Clowns. His mother saw him off at the station, giving him two sandwiches, two dollars, and two pairs of pants to take with him. His professional baseball career was about to begin.

Life with the Clowns wasn't easy. The travel by bus was tiring, and the food was poor. Furthermore, many of the older players ignored Henry at first. But he knew he had to stick, unless he wanted to return to Mobile.

He also had to break his habit of cross-handed hitting. Amazingly, he was already a top hitter and still used this incorrect technique. But once he tried it the right way, he found that he had even more power. He started cracking line drives all over the lot, and quickly became one of the stars of the team.

It wasn't long before Henry's reputation spread, and one day Boston Braves' scout Dewey Griggs was watching a doubleheader between the Clowns and Kansas City Monarchs in Buffalo. Griggs couldn't believe his eyes as he watched young Henry bang out seven hits in nine trips to the plate, including two homers, and also start five double-plays in the field.

Soon after, the Braves bought his contract for $10,000, but all Henry got out of it was a cardboard suitcase and a handshake from Clowns' owner Syd Pollock.

Henry went to Eau Claire, Wisconsin, of the Northern League, where he played in 87 games at the end of the 1952 season. He batted .336 with nine homers and sixty-one RBI's. Not bad for an eighteen year old. The Braves knew they had a good one, and the next season sent him to Jacksonville, Florida, of the South Atlantic League.

The Sally League, as it was called, had never had a black player. Henry was one of three blacks coming into the loop in 1953, just six years after Jackie Robinson broke the major league color line with the Dodgers. There were tough times. Fans were hostile in some cities, and Henry couldn't room with the rest of the team. Ironically, the blacks generally stayed in private homes and got better food and accommodations than the whites who stayed in hotels.

Henry said later, "There's only one way to break the color line, and that's with base hits. If you play really well, half the people don't remember what color you are."

He played well, all right, hitting .362 with 22 homers and 125 RBI's among his 208 hits. It looked as if he were about ready for the big time.

In October of that year, Henry married Barbara Lucas, who was a business student at Florida A & M University. The marriage took place on October 6, 1953, and two days later they had an unexpected, free honeymoon.

Ben Geraghty, the Jacksonville manager and a good friend to Henry, told him the Braves wanted to take a long look at him the next year. But they wanted an outfielder, not an infielder. So Henry spent the winter honeymooning and playing the outfield in the Puerto Rican League. And, in the spring of 1954, he was all set to try cracking the Braves' lineup.

The team had moved to Milwaukee by then, and Henry didn't expect he'd be playing much. Bobby Thomson, the old Giant, had come over in a trade and figured to be the third outfielder. The team already had some established and coming stars, men like Warren Spahn, Lew Burdette, Johnny Logan, Del Crandall, Billy Bruton, Eddie Mathews, and Joe Adcock. All of them were approaching their best playing years.

Young Henry wasn't seeing much action in the exhibition games. One day, he was drinking a coke under the stands after he had pinch hit. He watched as Bobby Thomson legged out a double. Thomson slid into second and never got up. His ankle was broken.

The next day, manager Charley Grimm approached Henry. He picked up the youngster's glove and tossed it to him.

"Here, kid. You're my new leftfielder. The job's yours until someone takes it away from you."

No one was about to take anything away from the young star out of Mobile. Henry played 122 games that year, hitting a solid .280, with 13 home runs and 69 RBI's. But his season ended early. On September 5, he slammed a triple against the Cincinnati Reds and caught his spikes sliding into third. He felt pain shoot up his leg. Now it was Henry's turn to have a broken ankle. It shelved him for the season.

Later, he told a reporter that he wasn't completely satisfied with his rookie year.

"I've been hitting .340 all my life," he said. "So hitting .280 with the Braves doesn't make me feel that good. I'd like to do better next year."

He did. Donning uniform number "44" for the first time, he played in all but one game, banging out 189 hits, 27 homers, and driving in 106 runs. His batting average was up to .314, and he was on his way.

So were the Braves. They finished second in 1955, then lost the pennant on the last day of the season in '56. That year, Henry won his first batting title with a .328 mark. He collected two hundred hits and led the league in doubles for the second straight season.

He was a rightfielder now, playing his position with smoothness and grace. At the plate, swinging right-handed, Aaron had a relaxed stance, slightly closed, midway in the box. The bat was held up and away, with his right elbow extended upward. His swing was a thing of beauty—a quick snap of his powerful wrists and the ball was on its way. Some say Aaron has the most powerful wrists of all time.

Midway through the 1957 season, the Braves traded for second baseman Red Schoendienst. He solidified the infield and was a fine number-two hitter. Henry was dropped into the clean-up spot and, batting fourth, led the league with 44 homers and 132 RBI's. His .322 batting average also helped lead the Braves to the National League pennant. In fact, Henry's all-around play earned him the Most Valuable Player Award for 1957.

In the World Series, Henry belted three homers and drove in seven runs with eleven hits and a .393 average. He also made a sensational catch in the field and supported the great pitching of Lew Burdette, who beat the Yanks three times, and the Braves were world champions.

Milwaukee won the pennant again the next year, but lost to the Yanks in the Series, despite another fine performance by Aaron. In 1959, the team lost a playoff to the Dodgers, with Henry winning another bat title with a .355 average. He had 39 homers that year, and 123 RBI's, but was nevertheless despondent about the team's loss.

"We lost on the final day in '56," he said, "then lost a playoff in '59. With a little luck, we'd have taken four straight pennants."

The trouble was that the Braves, as a team, were getting old. Only Henry kept up the pace. During the next four seasons he hit 40, 34, 45, and 44 homers, driving in 126, 120, 128, and 130 runs. He was really walloping the ball. When new manager Bobby Bragen suggested that he run more, he became a base-stealing threat, and, in 1963, became one of a handful of players to steal more than 30 bases (31) and hit more than 30 home runs (44) in a single season. He was also the National League's Player of the Year.

For a long time, Henry hadn't received due superstar recognition because of his smooth, effortless way of playing. But now, with the rest of the team slipping badly, he stood out like a gem in the forest. In 1966, the team moved to Atlanta, and Henry charmed a whole new set of baseball fans.

His average slipped to .279 that year, but he belted 44 homers and drove home 127 runs. He also hit the 400th circuit clout of his career that year, and the countdown began. Later in the same season, he and teammate Eddie Mathews set a record for most homers by two players on one team, 863, topping the old mark set by a couple of pretty fair sluggers, Babe Ruth and Lou Gehrig.

Now the Braves were starting to appreciate their 33-year-old leader. They gave Henry a two-year contract calling for $100,000 per year. He was an acknowledged superstar at last. He cracked thirty-nine homers that year, and, in 1968, blasted number five hundred off Mike McCormick of the Giants. He was now entering a select group of long-ball hitters.

Henry had never been considered quite on a par with the era's other two slugging outfielders, Mickey Mantle and Willie Mays, but suddenly he was gaining on both of them. He had never hit as many as fifty homers in a single season, but consistency was his byword. And the fans in his new city loved it.

"The fans in Atlanta are as great as those in Milwaukee during the pennant years," Henry said, "I can't remember ever getting a hand like the one when I hit my 500th homer. It was really great."

Others players in the league were also beginning to say just how good Henry Aaron was.

Sandy Koufax, the great Dodger lefty, said, "There's no

way you can pitch Henry when he's hot. He's the toughest in the league. Just Bad Henry, that's all."

Another superpitcher, Juan Marichal of the Giants, said the same thing. "That man. He beats you one way or he does it another way. But he always beats you."

And a long-time journeyman player, Charlie Lau, made a comparison after years of watching from the bench.

"I've seen all the top ones in both leagues," Lau said. "Mantle, Mays, Kaline, Mathews, Robinson, Clemente. I'll tell you, Aaron is the best. He beats you hitting, running, fielding, and stealing. There's nothing he can't do."

But when a newsman would mention all the records within Henry's reach, he'd just laugh.

"Setting records means you're getting old."

But he showed no signs of increasing age. In 1969, he led the Braves to the Western Division pennant in the National League with a .300 average, 44 homers, and 97 RBI's. Under the new setup, the Atlantans had to play the Eastern winner, the New York Mets, to get into the World Series.

Well, the Braves lost three straight, but Henry hit a homer in each of the games, drove in seven runs, and batted .357. As usual, he played his best in a crucial situation.

In 1970, more milestones came. He collected his 3,000th base hit, becoming the first player to combine that feat with 500 homers. (Since then, Willie Mays has also done it.) After getting the big hit, Henry said:

"It's been my goal for a long time. Now that I've reached 3,000 hits, everything else will fall into place. But it means quite a lot to me."

Henry was right. His achievements continued to mount. In 1971, he cracked his 600th homer off Gaylord Perry of the Giants. And what a year he had. As a 37-year-old player,

Hammerin' Hank batted .327, hit a career high of 47 homers, and drove home 118 runs.

The Braves showed their appreciation of his continued batting prowess. Before the 1972 season, he got his new, huge contract, and Atlanta team president Bill Bartholomay said, "He deserves every last penny of it."

Henry Aaron has always kept himself in shape. He is six feet tall, and his playing weight has always been about 180 pounds. He doesn't really look like a slugger. But, oh, those powerful wrists! In the last few years, he played a lot of first base. Many aging outfielders have done this. It saves the legs and enables them to concentrate on their hitting.

"I don't hit like I used to," Henry said recently. "I remember when I won the home run title in 1957, about 20 of my 44 were to right and right centerfield. Now I pull everything to left. I was probably a better all-around hitter then, but I'm not complaining."

Henry Aaron rarely complains. When he passed Willie Mays in career homers early in the 1972 season, it looked as if he were the only one with a chance to catch the Babe. Henry knows it, but hasn't let it faze him.

"I guess the pressure will be bad when I get close. But right now it's not bothering me too much."

Still, Henry's homers are the talk of baseball, and will continue to be for some time. Though he has never liked the limelight, there's no way he can avoid it now.

Since his mother gave him the two sandwiches, two dollars, and two pairs of pants when he left Mobile to join the Indianapolis Clowns in 1952, he has come a long way.

He may still like to think of himself as plain Henry Aaron, but to the rest of the sports world, Hammerin' Hank is a very extraordinary baseball player and human being.

SANFORD KOUFAX

Sandy

[1935–   ]

IN MANY RESPECTS, Sandy Koufax was an unlikely super-star. He had a dark, gentle, intelligent face, and didn't look like an athlete. His family placed great value on education and intellectual pursuits. And he was Jewish. For one reason or another, very few Jewish ballplayers have come to the ma-jors in the last couple of decades.

It took Sandy Koufax six long years to find himself as a pitcher. Lacking minor-league experience, and button-holed by a rule that prevented his being farmed out for seasoning, Sandy sat the Dodger bench, pitching occasionally, but un-able to get his game under control.

He was a southpaw flamethrower, as wild as he was fast. If he pitched one good inning, he'd pitch two bad ones. He showed occasional flashes of brilliance but more often was a study in futility. For the first six years of his career, the young lefty was a losing pitcher, compiling a 36–40 record. He was on the verge of quitting the game.

"Why don't the Dodgers get rid of Koufax," a disgruntled fan wrote to a Los Angeles paper. "He's excess baggage. He'll never be consistent and never really help the team. It's time for a change."

There was a change, all right. And if you didn't have eyes and see it for yourself, you'd think there was a different pitcher out there. And in effect, Sandy Koufax was a different pitcher. Almost overnight, he'd learned what pitching was all about.

In what can best be described as a second career, Sandy Koufax put together six seasons that rank among the greatest ever. His record for those years was 129–47. Three times he won more than twenty games. He became the only man in baseball history to pitch four no hitters, and one of them was a perfect game. He set numerous strikeout records and led the league with the lowest earned-run average five years in a row. He pitched in four World Series, and had an eight-game series ERA of 0.95.

Yet Sandy Koufax did all this despite two major ailments, the second of which caused premature retirement at the age of thirty-one. In his greatest years, he suffered his greatest tragedy. Success had been a long time coming, and when it finally did, it was cut short. But Koufax wasn't bitter. He became a Hall of Famer at age thirty-six, the youngest ever elected, and his pitching dominance from 1961 to 1966 will never be forgotten.

Today, Sandy Koufax is a happy man. He hadn't planned on a baseball career, although he was always an intense competitor on the mound. But when it ended, he accepted his fate without complaint.

Possessor of a blazing fastball, sharp-breaking curve, and effective change-up, Koufax combined these elements with fluid motion and outstanding stamina to flip goose-eggs at National League hitters. But his struggle for success was a long one. He worked for every inch, and he paid the price.

Sandy Koufax was born in Brooklyn, New York, on December 30, 1935. Only his name wasn't Sandy Koufax then. It was Sanford Braun. His parents divorced when he was three, and when his mother, Evelyn, remarried, Sandy chose to take the name of his new father, Irving Koufax.

While many stories about Koufax lead to the belief that he became a ballplayer because he had a good arm and nothing better to do, there's more to it than that. Sandy loved sports, right from the time he was a youngster. And he always did have the good arm.

"I found out about my arm when I was just a little kid," Sandy recalls. "We used to have snowball fights and I found I could get back so far that the other kids couldn't reach me. But I had no trouble reaching them. It was a pretty good way to win snowball fights."

And a pretty good way to play baseball, although the good arm usually resulted in young Sandy's being sent to the outfield by his coaches. Amazingly enough, he never pitched until he was fifteen, and didn't pitch regularly until two years after that.

Sandy had a happy childhood. Irving Koufax was a successful lawyer and the family was very comfortable. Sandy's mother seemed to want him to take after two of his uncles, both of whom were architects, but he showed no early tendencies toward studying. He'd rather be out playing ball.

First there had been the usual city games, like stoop ball and stick ball, and, of course, basketball. Before long, Sandy was one of the best basketball players in his neighborhood, and, at that time, he actually liked the court game better than baseball.

By the time he entered Lafayette High School, he was a basketball star. One time, several members of the New York

Knickerbockers came to the school to hold a clinic on the finer points of the game. The Knicks' top rebounder in those days, Harry "The Horse" Gallatin, told the boys he would show them how to dunk the ball.

Well, Harry must not have been feeling well that day, because he missed two dunks in a row. Suddenly, another of the Knicks, Al McGuire (now the coach at Marquette University), grabbed Sandy, who was a shade over six-feet tall, and said:

"Here's a kid who can show you how to do it."

Sandy's coach, Frank Rabinowitz, told McGuire that his star could dunk. Sandy responded to the pressure and rammed the ball through the hoop. Then he did it again! His teammates cheered and the other Knicks kidded Gallatin, who then took the youngster's name, and said:

"I'll be looking for you in the pro leagues some day."

Sandy was speechless. He couldn't remember ever feeling better or more proud. He continued to play and star, and when it came time to pick a college, it was his basketball ability that earned him a scholarship to the University of Cincinnati.

Why Cincinnati? Sandy doesn't really recall. He sort of flowed along with the tide in those days, perhaps because he wasn't really pushed. But he said good-by to his parents, who still hoped he'd be an architect, and packed off to college.

Though he was small for an inside man, he was nevertheless a rugged rebounder and had always played center or forward in high school. He played up front for the Bearcat freshman team and was the leading rebounder. He was also the third highest scorer with a 9.7 average. Then in the spring, something happened that was to change young Sandy Koufax's life.

Sandy found out that the baseball team would be making a southern swing during the spring. When he heard that New Orleans would be one of the stops, he figured that was the place to visit. So he looked up the Bearcat baseball coach and brazenly announced:

"Coach, you need another pitcher. I'm your man."

"What is this, Koufax?" the coach said. "I thought you were a basketball player?"

"I am, but I'm a baseball player, too. Done a lot of pitching on the New York sandlots. Matter of fact, I've had some offers to try out for the Phillies."

Sandy was telling the truth. He had played a lot of baseball on the sandlots, mostly because he loved sports, loved competing with the other boys. It wasn't that he loved baseball over everything else. But that good arm that he spoke about did the talking for him. He didn't have much control then. As he himself said: "I walked a lot of guys, and I struck out a lot of guys . . . every game."

Now there was another reason to play baseball . . . the trip south. So Sandy tossed a few fast ones and the coach knew the kid had it.

Sandy threw his blazer for the Bearcats that year. He had a 3–1 record with fifty-one strikeouts and thirty walks in thirty-one innings. That was about par for the course. Yet his tenure with the Cincinnati team served a useful purpose. It got him out in front of the scouts in a genuine competitive situation. There have been many players signed right off the sandlots, but pitching college ball helped put Sandy on the list of available talents.

Later, Sandy confided that he was never interested in playing baseball professionally until he learned he could get a bonus. But there were other reasons, too.

"I figured I was at Cincinnati just to play basketball," he said. "And all of a sudden I'm getting all these offers to try out for the majors. I began to feel that I owed it to myself to find out if I could really do it."

The bonus was important to him. When he was ready to sign his only condition was that the amount be large enough to pay for the rest of his education if he should return to school. Sandy was no dummy.

When his parents found out about the parade of offers, they were both astonished.

"Baseball!" they said in disbelief. "We thought you played basketball. What happened to that?"

But it was baseball now. In June, after school ended, Sandy was invited to the Polo Grounds to work out with the New York Giants. He was so nervous that he had absolutely no control, and the Jints lost interest. But the Pirates, Dodgers, and Phils were still in the running.

The Dodgers had taken a look at the young southpaw even before he went to Cincinnati. They liked his lively arm, in spite of his lack of control. Now Brooklyn scout Al Campanis wanted to take another look. He liked what he saw and the team made Sandy an offer.

From the Dodger standpoint, it was a good investment. Besides the fact that Sandy had ability, he was a local boy, right from Brooklyn, and he was Jewish. In a business sense, these factors could spin turnstiles. It was 1954, and people in the Brooklyn organization didn't know they'd be heading west in just three short years.

Sandy returned to Cincinnati, but he knew he had to make a decision. After constant talks with Campanis and his father, he decided to sign. He'd receive a salary of $6,000 and a bonus of $14,000. In the spring of 1955, Sandy Koufax was a

19-year-old rookie with the Brooklyn Dodgers.

It didn't matter that after he signed, better offers came from both the Pittsburgh Pirates and Milwaukee Braves. The deal was made and Sandy's big league career was about to begin.

Dodger pitching coach Joe Becker had his work cut out for him. Sandy was wild and still didn't have command of himself on the mound.

"His stride was wrong, he tried to throw too hard, and he just couldn't keep an easy, natural rhythm," said Becker. And no matter how much they worked with him, Sandy couldn't seem to correct the flaws.

One problem was in his basic build. On the mound, Sandy didn't look overpowering. But he was a good 6′ 2″ tall, and weighed around two hundred pounds. And he was deceptively strong. His back was a mass of muscle, almost too much muscle, in fact, because as soon as he'd tense up, all the muscles would tighten and he'd lose his good fastball. He could throw hard, but not fast. The ball didn't have that good "hop."

It's said that Dodger Manager Walter Alston once grabbed at Sandy's midsection to kid him about some excess fat. Alston suddenly jumped back in disbelief when he realized the slight bulge was a ridge of hard muscle.

Even when Sandy became a winning pitcher, Dodger trainers had to work on him before games to get those back muscles loose. And it wasn't unusual to see Sandy bending and stretching in the first few innings of a ball game.

All the bending and stretching didn't help much those first few years. As a rookie in 1955, Sandy got into just twelve games as the Dodgers rolled toward a pennant and their first World Series victory ever. He had a 2–2 record in forty-two innings, striking out thirty and walking twenty-eight along the way. His earned-run average was an even 3.00. But he showed enough flash to keep the Dodgers interested. Both his victories were complete game shutouts over Cincinnati and Pittsburgh. And against the Redlegs, he fanned 14 batters.

Still, it wasn't much. In '56, the Brooks won another pennant and Sandy did little to contribute, just sixteen games and a 2–4 mark. This time his earned run average ballooned to 4.88. It wasn't much.

The next year the Dodgers began using him more. He appeared in 34 games, posted a 5–4 record, and fanned 122 hitters in just 104 innings of pitching. His potential couldn't be ignored. The team moved to Los Angeles the next season, and Sandy celebrated with an 11–11 year, his best in the majors. But his ERA of 4.47 didn't help matters any. Then came 1959.

Sandy was just 8–6 that year, but a couple of things happened that were very encouraging. Pitching against the Giants on August 31, Sandy Koufax tied a major league record by striking out eighteen men. He was throwing his blazer and controlling it. He walked just two, and the 82,000 fans in the Los Angeles Coliseum went wild. He had struck out thirteen in his previous start and also set a two-game standard of thirty-one strikeouts. It reached 41 when he fanned 10 in his next start.

It prompted Manager Alston to give him a World Series start that year against the Chicago White Sox. Sandy pitched a brilliant game, but lost it, 1–0, on two singles and a double-play grounder. It was a tough loss, but Sandy was happy with his season. He thought he had finally found himself as a pitcher.

Then 1960 turned into a disaster. Koufax fell to 8–13 with a 3.91 ERA. He had 197 strikeouts in 175 innings, but he was erratic and undependable. It was beginning to look as if he'd never make a consistent pitcher.

Sandy himself was quite discouraged. He'd thought he was out of the woods with the 8–6 season in 1959. So when he slipped again in '60, he thought for the first time of calling it quits.

And he might have, too, if it hadn't been for Norm Sherry. Norm was the Dodger's third-string catcher and never had much of a major league career. His brother Larry had a few good years as a Dodger reliever and starred in the '59 series, but Norm just hung on awhile before dropping out.

He and Sandy were friends, and he watched the lefthander's struggle intently. One day in spring training before the 1961 season, he decided to have a talk with Sandy.

It was right before a game in which Sandy was to pitch for the Dodger "B" squad, composed of rookies and second liners. Sherry was the catcher.

"Hey, Sandy. Let's try something today," Norm said. "Just relax out there. Don't try to blow the ball past everybody. Throw it with an easier motion. And use your curve and change-up more. Don't be afraid to be a pitcher."

The game started, and pretty soon Sandy was mowing down the opposition. His control was good and he was still getting strikeouts. The one time he got into a jam, Sherry trotted out to the mound.

"OK, this is where you're tensing up," the catcher said. "I can feel it already. Listen, that ball of yours is getting to the plate just as fast without you killing yourself. Just pitch to the spots and the rest will take care of itself."

Sandy listened, and he won the game. Later, he told Sherry

that he actually felt good on the mound. The formula seemed to work. And what Sherry said about the Koufax fastball was true. Without all the tensing up and straining, Sandy was throwing just about as fast, and the ball had more natural movement, more hop.

Throughout the spring, Sandy worked on the new delivery, and concentrated on relaxing. Manager Alston and the Dodger coaches were amazed. They put him in the regular starting rotation.

Suddenly, Sandy was a winner. Pitching in a regular turn for the first time in his career, he won 10 of his first 13 games, including six complete-game victories in a row. He tired somewhat in the second half, but when the 1961 season was over, Sandy had won 18 and lost just 13. His ERA was still high at 3.52, but he'd struck out 269 batters in 256 innings, and walked just 96. He couldn't wait for the next season to begin.

He started the 1962 season as if there were no stopping him. On June 30, Sandy had a 10–4 record and was facing the New York Mets. Throwing hard and mixing in his curve and change-up, he pitched the first no-hitter of his career, striking out 13 Mets en route. He was getting better and better.

But even in his greatest moment, there was trouble. He had broken an artery in the fleshy part of his hand some time before, and now the circulation to his left index finger was being impaired. In fact, the finger was numb the night he threw the no hitter. Three more victories followed, bringing his record to 14–4. Then the finger really got bad.

Blood circulation to the index finger was cut off. For a short time, doctors thought Sandy might lose the finger. But it slowly began to improve. He even tried a few late-season starts, though he had little and finished with a 14–7 mark, and a big question mark for the next year.

One thing was certain now. When healthy, Sandy Koufax was becoming one of the best pitchers in the National League. Pitching in 184 innings in 1962, he struck out 216 hitters and walked just 57. The old wildness was gone.

When he reported to spring training in 1963, everyone had the same question.

"How's the finger, Sandy?"

"It seems just fine," he'd answer.

Indeed it was. The circulation had returned over the winter, and the doctors said it shouldn't bother him any more. It didn't. That season, Sandy Koufax really blossomed. Free from physical ailments, he was superb.

When the year ended, Sandy had a record of 25–5. He had set a major league mark for lefthanders with 11 shutouts, three of them coming in a row at one point. He threw his second no hitter, this one against the Giants, struck out 306 batters in 311 innings, and he walked just 58. His earned-run average was a league-leading 1.88.

In the World Series against the mighty New York Yankees, Sandy contributed two victories in a four-game Dodger sweep. He fanned fifteen Bombers (then a record) in the first game, and won the fourth with ease. He was named the National League's Most Valuable Player and won the Cy Young Award as the best pitcher in baseball.

Sandy was not yet twenty-eight years old when the 1963 season ended. By most standards, he was at his pitching peak. Experts predicted another five to seven years of top-flight hurling from the lefthander with the fluid motion and blazing fastball. But you never know in sports.

The next three seasons, 1964 to 1967, Sandy Koufax was to

compile records of 19–5, 26–8, and 27–9. On the sur-
face, that sounds great. But those three years were filled with
pain and suffering from the condition that would force his
early retirement at thirty-one.

Sandy was pitching his customary sensational ball in 1964.
He'd already hurled his third no hitter and had set a major
league mark with ten or more strikeouts in 55 games. Then
on August 8, against Milwaukee, Sandy dove back into second base on a pickoff attempt and landed hard on his left
elbow. His usual post-game soreness became even worse.

On August 20, he topped the Cards, 3–0, striking out
thirteen and running his record to 19–5. But when he
awoke the next morning, he couldn't believe the sight that
greeted him. Sandy tells it in his own words.

"I had to drag my arm out of bed like a log. That's what it
looked like, a log. A water-logged log. Where it had been
swollen outside the joint before, it was now swollen all the
way from the shoulder down to the wrist—inside, outside,
everywhere. For an elbow, I had a knee; that's how thick it
was."

Doctors immediately ran a barrage of tests. When the results were in, Sandy heard the verdict. He was suffering from
traumatic arthritis in the elbow. It was a condition brought
on by the wear and tear of pitching. The cartilage was being
chipped away gradually. The incident in Milwaukee may
have hastened it, but it probably would have happened anyway. The bad part was that the condition was irreversible. It
would continue to get worse.

When the arm acted up in the spring of 1965, it looked as
if he had a real problem. Then Sandy made a suggestion. Perhaps he should skip throwing between starts, giving the arm
more time to recover. He tried it and it worked. Pitching

only in games, he hurled 336 innings, the most of his career, set an all-time record of 382 strikeouts, had an ERA of 2.04, a record of 26–8, and pitched the Dodgers to another pennant. It was obvious that he was still the best pitcher in baseball.

He set another record in 1965. He became the only player in history to pitch four no-hit games. And the fourth was a gem. He defeated the Chicago Cubs on September 9, and faced just twenty-seven batters. It was a perfect game. When it ended, the Cubs' Ernie Banks was amazed.

"Koufax just tried to throw the ball past us . . . and he did!"

Once again, Sandy was a World Series hero, winning twice against the Minnesota Twins, including the decisive seventh game, when he shut out the Twins with only two days rest. It was hard to believe that this man had a bad elbow.

But it was bad. Sandy often had to take pain killers after a game. He had many sleepless nights, and often had to have the elbow drained. His opponents couldn't believe it, because he pitched so well against them, but as Sandy said, pitching seemed to relieve the elbow temporarily. He had no pain when he threw his blazer. It was between starts that the agony set in.

By now, Sandy was becoming a wealthy man. He had a $125,000 contract and had won his second Cy Young Award. He began to think about retiring.

The 1966 season had the same results on the field. A super season. His record was 27–9. He fanned 317 batters and had an ERA of 1.73. His third 300-strikeout season was another record, and he pitched the Dodgers to another pennant.

He didn't have much luck in the Series. The Orioles swept the Dodgers in four games. Sandy lost one, but was hurt by several Dodger errors. Still, he won his third Cy Young Award and the average fan had no idea what was about to happen.

Just two months after the season ended, Sandy called a press conference. He shocked the sports world by announcing he was quitting baseball.

He explained about his arm, about the pain, the needles, the pills, the whole routine he had been living for two years. He also said that the arm was beginning to shorten, and he found that he couldn't reach his face when he shaved without bending over.

"Let's say I've had a few too many shots and pills because of this arm. I just don't want to take a chance of disabling myself. I have no regrets for one minute of my twelve years in the big leagues, but I could regret one season too many.

"What I'm saying is that I want to live the rest of my life with complete use of my body."

That was it. Two months after shutting out the Twins with just two days' rest, and after having pitched 659 innings in two years, never missing a regular turn, Sandy's arm could take no more. Sure, he might have gone on, might even have turned in a few more spectacular years, but the doctors warned him of the eventual consequences. The arm was deteriorating. His decision took courage, but it was the rational and intelligent thing to do.

Today, Sandy is a Hall of Famer and a broadcaster for NBC. He's married to the former Anne Widmark, daughter of actor Richard Widmark, and living in Los Angeles. He's a happy, contented man, with no regrets.

But it will be a long time before people forget Sandy Koufax, left-handed pitcher supreme. He was *the pitcher* of the 1960's, dominating the game as thoroughly as any hurler ever has. And all because he learned to relax.

INDEX

BILL GUTMAN

When Bill Gutman entered Washington College in Chester-town, Maryland, he wanted to become a dentist. When he graduated in 1965, he had a B.A. in English Literature and thoughts about a career in writing.

After a year of graduate work at the University of Bridge-port, Mr. Gutman became a reporter and feature writer for the Greenwich *Times*, in Connecticut. Before long he was the paper's sports editor.

A brief fling in the advertising world convinced him to write full time. He began freelancing and has written both fiction and non-fiction for many sports magazines. He is the author of a biography of basketball star Pistol Pete Maravich, and has written books on all the major sports. He is currently a contributing editor for *Superstar Sports* magazine.

A native of New York City, Bill Gutman grew up in Con-necticut and presently lives in Ridgefield with his wife, Eliza-beth.